KU-726-108

WESTLAND
LYNX

1976 to present (HAS Mk.2, Mk.3 and HMA Mk.8 models)

COVER IMAGE: Westland Lynx HMA Mk.8.
(Mike Badrocke)

© Lee Howard 2016

All rights reserved. No part of this publication may be reproduced or stored in a retrieval system or transmitted, in any form or by any means, electronic, mechanical, photocopying, recording or otherwise, without prior permission in writing from Haynes Publishing.

First published in July 2016

A catalogue record for this book is available from the British Library.

ISBN 978 0 85733 814 3

Library of Congress control no. 2015948106

Published by Haynes Publishing,
Sparkford, Yeovil,
Somerset BA22 7JJ, UK.
Tel: 01963 440635
Int. tel: +44 1963 440635
Website: www.haynes.co.uk

Haynes North America Inc.
861 Lawrence Drive,
Newbury Park, California 91320, USA.

Printed in Malaysia.

Copy editor: Michelle Tilling
Proof reader: Penny Housden
Indexer: Peter Nicholson
Page design: James Robertson

Acknowledgements

In producing this book the author would like to extend his gratitude to the following individuals and organisations, without whose help and assistance it would not have been possible:

AgustaWestland Ltd; Lt Rich Bell, RN; Marcus Brakes; Mick Burrow; Cdr Louis Wilson-Chalon RN; Brian Davies; Lt Cdr Lee Davies, RN; DE&S Lynx Wildcat Project Team; Lt Rob Dixon, RN; Lt Mike Doyle, RN; Lt Mike Emptage, RN; Jonathan Falconer; Lt Mark Finnie, RN; the staff of the Archives Department of the Fleet Air Arm Museum, especially Barbara Gilbert and Catherine Cooper; Jason 'Fluff' Freeman; David Gibbings; Jack Gibbs; Lt Cdr Brett Gillies, RN; Cdr Al Haigh, RN; Lt Jonny Hamlyn, RN; Lt Andrew Henderson, RN; Lt Cdr Peter Higgins, RN; Neil Irvine; Lt Cdr Bill Lauste, RN; Lynx Wildcat Maritime Force; Steve Mather; Graham Mercer; Cdr Philip Tilden, RN and the ship's company of HMS *Monmouth*; the late Eric Myall; Lt Trystram Negus, RN; CPO Laura O'Neill; PO Tim Rowe; Geoff Russell; CPO James Simons; Lt Cdr Alex Sims, RN; Lt A.J. Thompson, RN; the late Dave Williams; Lt Simon Wilson, RN; Lt Cdr Chris Yelland, RN.

I would also like to give particular thanks to the Commanding Officer of 815 Naval Air Squadron, Cdr Phil Richardson, RN and the members of 815 Naval Air Squadron 229 Flight: Lt Cdr Simon 'Sharkey' Ward, RN, Lt Keith Webb, RN, CPO Matthew 'Cakey' Eccles, PO Dave Downing, PO Dan Joy, LH Scotty Latham, AET Micky Collins, LH Rory Lowther, AET Chris 'Meds' Meadows and LAC Sev Holbrook.

WESTLAND
LYNX

1976 to present (HAS Mk.2, Mk.3 and HMA Mk.8 models)

Owners' Workshop Manual

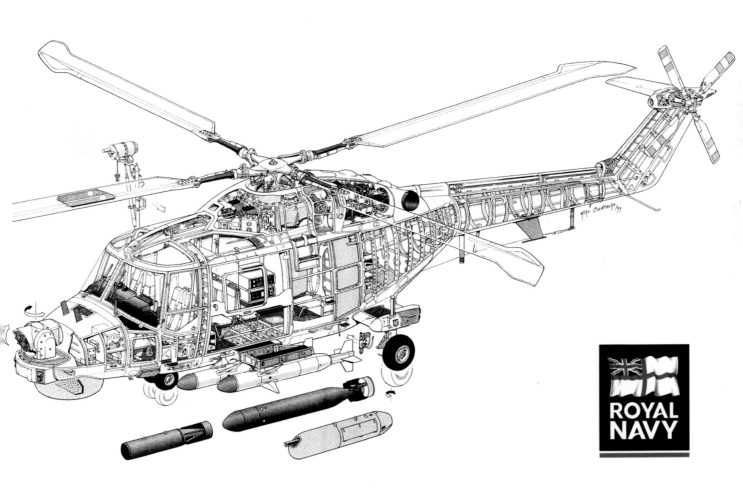

An insight into the design, construction, operation and maintenance of the Royal Navy's multi-role ship-borne helicopter

Lee Howard

Three Lynx HMA Mk.8s of 815 NAS 'B' Section and HQ Flight together with a Lynx HAS Mk.3ICE of 815 NAS 212 Flight, HMS *Endurance*, in formation, 10 July 2009. *(Author)*

Contents

Introduction

Although the United Kingdom can still proudly boast that it is one of the world's major helicopter manufacturers, owing to the increasing collaboration with other European companies the Westland Lynx can rightfully stake its claim as the last mass-produced military helicopter of all-British original basic design.

In military service for over 40 years with the British Armed Forces, this agile, multi-role combat helicopter has seen service all around the world and in every type of operational theatre – from the frozen wastes of Antarctica to the heat of the Gulf and the Caribbean, being involved in wars, providing humanitarian assistance, conducting geological surveys, and engaging in counter-narcotics, counter-piracy and counter-terrorism roles.

This book focuses primarily on the Royal Navy's ship-borne HMA Mk.8 variant – itself a development of the earlier HAS Mk.2 and HAS Mk.3, which began entering service with the Fleet Air Arm in 1976. Many of the components and systems are, however, common to the variants operated by the type's other operating British military air arm: the Army Air Corps. In 2017, the HMA Mk.8 variant will become the last of the Rolls-Royce Gem-powered Lynx in British military service, bringing to an end an illustrious 41 years of operations with the Royal Navy.

OPPOSITE Fast, sleek, agile: the Westland Lynx HMA Mk.8 and its predecessors has served the Royal Navy for over 40 years. *(All pictures credited to the author, unless otherwise stated)*

LEFT Former Westland Chief Test Pilot Colin Hague MBE and Lieutenant James Woods, RN, cutting the special cake made to commemorate the 40th anniversary of the Lynx's first flight and the 25th anniversary of achieving the World Speed Record, 2011. *(Crown Copyright)*

Chapter One

Developing helicopters for small-ship operations

Today, helicopter operations from small ships are commonplace and, as such, are largely taken for granted. Having assumed the lead in developing the helicopter anti-submarine and anti-surface warfare concepts during and immediately after the Second World War, the Royal Navy blazed a trail that other navies throughout the world have followed ever since. Many countries' frigates and destroyers are now equipped with variants of the ubiquitous Westland Lynx.

OPPOSITE Sikorsky R-4 Hoverfly I FT835 operating from the makeshift deck on board MV *Daghestan* during transit from the USA to Britain, 1943. *(via Phil Butler)*

Although the potential for the helicopter to provide an anti-submarine warfare (ASW) capability was uppermost in the thoughts of the British Admiralty when taking the decision to place an order for a small number of Sikorsky R-4 Hoverflies from the USA in 1943 – a period later known as the Battle of the Atlantic – the realities at that time were somewhat different. Helicopters were still very much in their infancy and their development had been hampered by the diversion of money and manpower to their fixed-wing counterparts for the waging of war. The only powerplants available were piston engines, which either produced insufficient power or were too large and too heavy. Unlike fixed-wing aircraft, of course, helicopters have no wings as an additional means of generating the lift required to offset the weight of their engines. As a result, the aircraft were woefully underpowered, and this meant that they had no load-lifting capability – and indeed did not have cabin space for equipment anyway. Not being able to carry much fuel, they also lacked range.

Nonetheless, it was clear to some of the forward-thinking individuals in the Admiralty, however, that what they did provide was a means of training aircrew in the relatively new art of rotary-wing aviation. This gave them

the benefit of being in the best position to take advantage of future improved designs in development that *did* have the capability to undertake ASW roles.

But it would not be until the 1950s, with the introduction of these more capable – although still far from ideal – designs that the conceptual evolution of helicopter operations at sea could really begin.

Gradually, other Royal Navy ships such as cruisers and destroyers were adapted with landing platforms and even, in some cases, hangars to enable the operation and safe carriage of helicopters. Once the concept had been effectively proven, attention finally began to drift towards the real advantages of small-ship helicopter operations.

Engine development

A recurring theme with regard to the development of helicopters – particularly small helicopters – was the lack of government investment in small gas turbine engines. Up until the late 1950s the only powerplants available were large, heavy, predominantly radial piston engines adapted from existing designs fitted to fixed-wing aircraft. Buried within the fuselage

BELOW Fairey Ultralight G-AOUK being flown by Fairey Chief Test Pilot Ron Gellatly who would later go on to carry out the first flight of the WG-13. *(via Fred Ballam)*

structure where they took up large amounts of space, these air-cooled engines relied upon heavy fan assemblies in order to keep them cool and also required clutch and freewheel units to provide a means of engaging and disengaging with the main rotor drive. All of this added complexity meant that they gave poor power-to-weight performance. With the introduction of kerosene-powered jet aircraft at sea during the 1950s, it also meant that two different types of fuel had to be carried on board with all of the inherent dangers and additional infrastructure needed to support that.

What was called for was an altogether different type of engine. One which was small – yet powerful – and which used the same type of fuel as other embarked aircraft types.

Fairey Ultralight

In the late 1950s, the Fairey Aviation Company designed and built a number of prototype concept helicopters called the Ultralight. Powered by a single Blackburn Palouste gas turbine engine, these diminutive aircraft (which were only 15ft long) had main rotors driven by hot gases directed from the engine to the rotor tips – so-called tip jets. Trials aboard HMS *Grenville* in

the English Channel in February 1957 and aboard HMS *Undaunted* the following year demonstrated to the Royal Navy the potential value of small-ship helicopter operations. But the Ultralight was ultimately too small and lacked sufficient range to be a serious contender.

Blackburn Turmo

The year 1957 was something of a watershed for British helicopter design. That summer, Blackburn had been awarded a type-test certificate for the Turmo gas turbine engine, the licence production rights for which they had acquired from Turbomeca of France five years earlier. The Turmo gave rise to the potential for producing a more capable replacement for the diminutive Saunders-Roe Skeeter which, in September of that year, had formed the rotary-wing element of the newly formed Army Air Corps (AAC).

Saunders-Roe P-531

Although it would give the AAC an appreciation of the usefulness of the helicopter in a modern battlefield armoury, the Skeeter's development had been protracted and

ABOVE The diminutive Saunders-Roe Skeeter AOP.12 – seen here during a visit to Yeovil – was woefully underpowered and gave rise to the requirement for a suitable replacement for the AAC.
(AgustaWestland)

the performance limitations afforded by its in-line de Havilland Gipsy Major piston engine had restricted it to operations in the cooler European theatres. At the time, however, the British Army were becoming heavily involved in the policing of many former British dependencies that were in both hotter and higher climes.

This performance limitation led to the issue of requirements for a Unit Light Helicopter (ULH) and a Light Utility Helicopter (LUH). The ULH requirement was eventually met by the piston-engined Westland Sioux (itself a licence-built version of the successful American design, the Bell 47, built jointly by Agusta in Italy and Westland at Yeovil). The successful development of the Blackburn Turmo, meanwhile, became the catalyst for the much-needed redesign of the Skeeter, emerging as the Nimbus gas turbine-engined Saunders-Roe P-531.

Using many common parts, the new P-531 emerged in the summer of 1958 at the company's Eastleigh works. Although the first two aircraft were civil-registered private-venture prototypes, the third, fourth and fifth examples were completed as P-531 O/N navalised versions, resplendent in Royal Navy markings.

Later versions were completed as Army variants, eventually becoming the Westland Scout that would satisfy the Army's LUH requirement.

Although the company had originally chosen to christen the P-531 O/N as the 'Seraph', during deck-landing trials with 700 Naval Air Squadron aboard the destroyer HMS *Undaunted* the following year, the name 'Sea Sprite' was used unofficially. Both of these were soon dropped and the final, much-refined production aircraft was named the Westland Wasp, entering service with the Fleet Air Arm in 1963. The Wasp was an extremely successful helicopter, seeing service with the Royal Navy for a quarter of a century before being finally replaced by the Lynx in 1988. Those 25 years had cemented the small helicopter's place as an indispensable asset for the surface fleets of navies throughout the world.

Design considerations

In designing a helicopter for operations from small ships, one has to bear in mind several factors. One particularly important consideration, not surprisingly, is size.

LEFT The first production Westland Wasp HAS Mk.1, XS463, being flown by Westland Test Pilot John Morton using the rolling deck platform at RAE Bedford to simulate deck landing at sea. *(AgustaWestland)*

The ability of a fighting ship – such as a frigate or destroyer – to carry aircraft is naturally secondary to its main role. But providing protection for the aircraft from the harsh salt water environment when not flying and a space in which to conduct essential maintenance means that the construction of a hangar becomes essential, together with a flight deck from which to operate. Studies would show typical weight penalty figures incurred by the addition of a rudimentary hangar facility for a helicopter of 2,500kg all-up weight (AUW) to be in the range of 80 tonnes of additional superstructure through to 250 tonnes for a 12,000kg aircraft. Larger aircraft would also require more personnel to both fly and maintain it, especially during round-the-clock operations, meaning more space for accommodation would be needed on board, too.

To help reduce the size of an on-board hangar, ways of reducing the overall dimensions of such a helicopter have to be employed. For instance, the ability to fold the main rotor blades reduced the overall width, while designing a folding tail would allow for a reduction in overall length.

BELOW Flight deck personnel remove the lashings holding Westland Wasp HAS Mk.1, XT432, of HMS *Hecate* Flight, to the deck prior to launch. The Wasp proved the concept of operating small helicopters from Royal Navy frigates. *(AgustaWestland)*

Chapter Two

The Lynx story

The story of the Westland Lynx can be traced as far back as October 1963, when a series of project studies were carried out by the Westland Aircraft Company into the design and development of a small, tactical twin-engined helicopter – not for the Royal Navy, but for the Army Air Corps.

OPPOSITE An early artist's impression of the WG.13 Naval variant. *(AgustaWestland)*

In the early 1960s, the Army Air Corps' helicopter inventory consisted of the piston-engined Saunders-Roe Skeeter and Bell 47 Sioux, as well as the turbine-powered Westland Scout and Sud-Aviation Alouette. Increasingly, however, the British Army found themselves being sent to help with the policing of several British colonies that were in the process of being handed back to independent rule; many of these were in locations where the hot and often high conditions precluded the use of the Skeeter (which never operated any further away from the UK than Germany) and both the Sioux and Scout had little in the way of cabin capacity to carry troops or equipment. As a consequence, they were relegated to training and airborne observation post (AOP) roles.

A requirement – Naval, General and Air Staff Target (NGAST) OR.3335 – was raised for a small 'squad carrier', twin-engined, light tactical helicopter for the Army with a flight crew of two, capable of carrying up to ten armed men. It would need to be tough and simple enough to 'live' in the field alongside the troops, quick and simple to maintain, highly reliable, capable of speeds up to 160 knots, easily manoeuvrable on the ground and easy to rebuild after air transportation.

Westland Aircraft Ltd (WAL) at Yeovil responded to the requirement with a proposal allocated the company project designation WG-3. This marked a significant change in strategy for Westland. Since its entry into the field of rotary-wing production in 1947, the company's production output had been purely in the form of manufactured licence-built examples of original Sikorsky designs from the USA. Even the short-lived private-venture Westland Westminster project of 1958–60 utilised major components borrowed from Sikorsky. It had proved to be a shrewd move: the utilisation of technology already tried and tested by the Americans – known as technology transfer – effectively negated the need for prohibitively expensive and time-consuming trials programmes, which would otherwise render such a venture commercially unviable. Westland could, instead, devote their efforts and resources to developing and improving on these existing designs and target a burgeoning foreign small-helicopter market.

In stark contrast, the other contemporary

British helicopter manufacturers – Bristol, Fairey and Cierva – had all chosen to base their production on the post-war government 'protectionist' policy of 'buying British'. Effectively bankrupt after the Second World War and saddled with huge debts – notably to the USA – the government were keen to maximise the export of British products in order to begin to reduce its financial deficit. An incentive to this was the promise of essential Ministry of Supply (MoS) Research and Development funding to underpin their work and a guarantee that no contracts would be placed for any foreign-competitor designs. Purchases from abroad normally had to be paid for in US dollars, which Britain could not afford. The allure of producing indigenous helicopter designs – restimulating the aviation industry and having the British market to themselves – was too attractive.

Westland, however, thought otherwise. Most of the patents for helicopter technology were held by American companies and these would be costly to negotiate the use of. The time and effort involved in having to effectively redo all of the research and development to achieve the same output that the Americans already had was deemed pointless. By entering into the licence agreement, Westland could leapfrog their competition in one fell swoop and be in mass helicopter production almost immediately.

And that is precisely what happened. By marketing the Anglicised version of the Sikorsky S-51 for the domestic and foreign civil market and as the Dragonfly for the military – providing British jobs – Westland had in effect circumvented the MoS Indigenous Procurement Plan. Starting with the Fleet Air Arm in 1949, the British armed forces began procuring Westland Dragonflies to meet their service needs, while the Bristol and Fairey designs were still very much in development.

WG-3

The WG-3 proposal consisted of a helicopter powered by a pair of Pratt & Whitney PT.6A gas turbines producing 720shp each. Quickly up-issued to WG-3A – utilising a modified Whirlwind main rotor gearbox fitted within a pillar in the rear of the cabin – allowed a modified rear four-bladed rotor from a Bristol

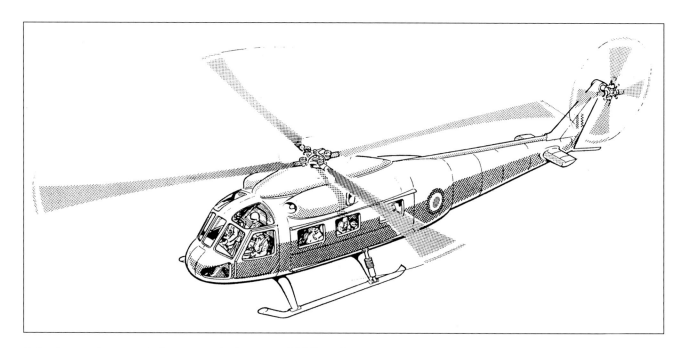

Belvedere tandem rotor helicopter to sit almost flush with the cabin roof. This reduced the overall height of the aircraft to tie in with the air transportability requirement, while also taking advantage of components that had already undergone testing on other types.

The Army, however, insisted on the aircraft being capable of lifting a Land Rover vehicle, forcing Westland to make the WG-3A stronger. This led to a weight increase that ultimately required engines developing 800shp each; at the time, however, no such engine designs were available. The alternative WG-3C variant would have been fitted with a pair of 1,200shp Gnome engines, increasing the aircraft's all-up mass (AUM) to 11,100lb and enabling it to carry up to 14 troops plus a commander and the two flight crew. This power increase, however, would also have exceeded the design limits of the gearbox.

The twin-engined WG-3B saw the proposal for the replacement of the Whirlwind gearbox with yet more components from within the parent company's existing inventory: a Bristol Sycamore gear train.

By late 1963, however, the decision was taken to discontinue the WG-3 design, which had become too complicated. The size of the aircraft had also begun to encroach on the work being undertaken for a Wessex replacement. Therefore, to avoid any confusion with work that had already been carried out, all further work was reassigned to the new design number WG-13.

WG-13

With the acquisition of the rotary-wing assets from Fairey Aviation during the painful amalgamation and rationalisation of the British aircraft industry in 1960, Westland had found itself in the powerful position of being not only the sole British helicopter manufacturer, but also the inheritor of a substantial amount of invaluable helicopter design expertise. Much of this had been gained as a result of the earlier absorption of the former Cierva and Saunders-Roe helicopter design teams who had done a great deal of the pioneering pre- and post-war work in rotary-wing development. With their Yeovil factory busily churning out the Anglicised Sikorsky licence-built designs such as the Whirlwind and Wessex, the initial design work for the newly retitled WG-13 project was handed over to the former Fairey Hayes Division in Middlesex.

Design work on an 8,000lb aircraft continued throughout 1964 with the WG-13A featuring shoulder-mounted engines ahead of the main gearbox; WG-13B with PT-6 engines and two-stage Whirlwind gearbox mounted above the cabin; and WG-13D and WG-13E with twin 700shp Continental T-72 engines mounted aft of the main gearbox. The T-72 was some 60lb lighter than the PT.6 and consumed less fuel.

The skid undercarriage-equipped WG-13F featured a structural spine to carry the main

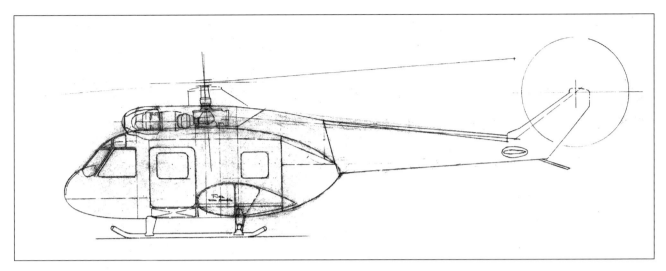

ABOVE Drawings of the WG-13F with external strengthening.
(AgustaWestland)

BELOW WG-13-J with stub-wing arrangement.
(AgustaWestland)

aerodynamic loads, thus allowing a larger cabin door aperture to be incorporated. The spine also doubled as a fuel tank.

The WG-13J was perhaps the most radical of the early designs with streamlined cockpit and wide-bodied fuselage. It also featured a shoulder-mounted stub wing.

The WG-13R was an armed escort variant with a tandem crew of Pilot and Gunner, retractable skid undercarriage and was fitted with a pair of 770shp Continental T-72 engines positioned aft of the main rotor gearbox.

The WG-13S was another armed escort version carrying 2,500lb of weapons and armour and capable of speeds up to 180 knots. The WG-13Q was to have been a Utility variant, complete with chin-mounter turret for defensive fire.

The designs finally started to gel when, in April 1966, consideration was given to the production of the two common variants – the Armed Reconnaissance and the Utility – together with a civil and a Naval variant modified for deck landing. These would be

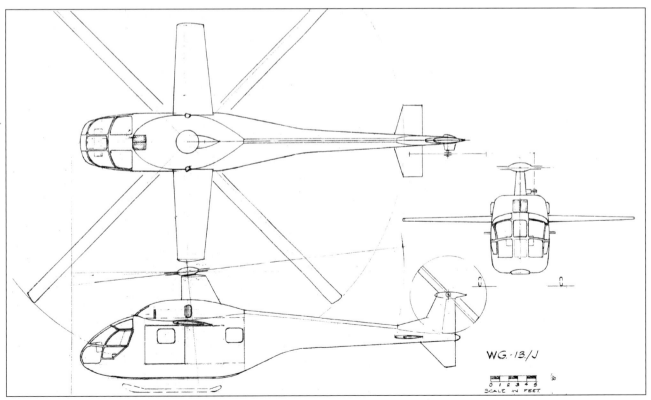

WG·13/J

0 1 2 3 4 5
SCALE IN FEET

designated as the WG-13T, WG-13U, WG-13V and WG-13W respectively.

The WG-13T Armed Reconnaissance Helicopter represented perhaps the greatest departure from the original WG-13 design. With a crew of three – a Gunner in the extreme nose with Pilots seated side by side above and behind – the design featured enclosed weapon bays in the belly, a chin-mounted gun and a retractable skid-type undercarriage. A further iteration of the T-variant had a retractable wheeled undercarriage with weapons mounted on short swept stub wings, while another had a crew of just two with fixed skid undercarriage and a deep – almost rectangular – cross-section fuselage.

Royal Navy interest

At this time, the Royal Navy was also actively looking at the future upgrade or replacement of their Westland Wasp helicopter, which by now had been in service for three years. The aircraft had proved to be popular and had further cemented the usefulness of small helicopters embarked on small ships. It was, however, hindered by its relatively poor range, its single Nimbus engine and its restricted weapon load.

To be able to fit on to the current fleet of ships, the WG-13's main rotor span needed to be reduced to a maximum of 44ft. At an AUM of 8,000lb and fitted with two Continental T-72 engines, the poor single-engined performance was such that a greater rotor span was required in order to achieve autorotation safely.

In June 1966 a Joint Service Requirement was issued, together with the Anglo-French requirement to collaborate on three of the WG-13 designs: the Naval variant for the Royal Navy and French Navy; the Utility variant for the British Army; and the Armed Reconnaissance variant for the French Army only.

Choosing an engine

Like the Royal Navy, the French Navy had their own requirements for main rotor diameter, asking instead to further reduce this to 42½ft, further compounding the engine issue.

In the original design proposal for this twin gas turbine-engined, Multi-Purpose Helicopter (Utility), the Westland WG-13 was to be powered by a pair of 750shp Astazou XIV or 770shp Continental T-72 engines with the latter being licence-built by Rolls-Royce. In September 1966, discussions between Rolls-Royce, Bristol-Siddeley Engines and Continental led to the realisation that the T-72 would not be suitable after all and that, with no other acceptable powerplant available, a whole new engine design would be required for the WG-13. And so was born the Bristol-Siddeley BS.360 free-turbine turboshaft engine which would eventually become the Rolls-Royce Gem.

Designing and developing a new engine from scratch at this stage in the helicopter's

ABOVE The first of the BS.360 engines being assembled at Leavesden. *(RRHT)*

BELOW Final assembly of the now retitled RS.360 engine at Leavesden showing the compact nature of the design. *(Rolls-Royce Heritage Trust)*

development was an extremely risky proposal and provoked much concern within Westland. Rolls-Royce, however, managed to give sufficient reassurances that they would be able to meet the development timescales. In March 1967 a pair of BS.360-07 engines, rated initially at 800shp, were put forward for the WG-13 programme and it was duly endorsed as the chosen powerplant for the aircraft.

Collaboration

The late 1960s marked an unprecedented era of multinational aviation project collaboration: the civil Concorde programme and the military Jaguar and MRCA (Multi-Role Combat Aircraft – later to become Tornado) designs. On 22 February 1967 a Memorandum of Understanding (MoU) on helicopter collaboration was signed between the French and the British, which as well as the Lynx would ultimately lead to the Gazelle and Puma helicopter designs used by both countries.

A series of models of the WG-13 designs were displayed by Westland at the 1967 Paris Air Show. These included the radically different French Army Armed Reconnaissance variant with a single 20mm cannon or twin machine guns fitted in a chin turret, short stub wings capable of carrying six AS11 or two AS12 missiles and featuring a tailwheel arrangement which utilised the common rotor system.

In July 1967, the formal Intention to Proceed (ITP) was given for the production of the prototype aircraft. Initially some 17 flying examples were planned to be built as part of the trials programme:

- 5 Basic models for testing of airframe and component reliability
- 3 Utility for the Army trials
- 3 Armed Reconnaissance for the French Army
- 4 Naval variants for the French Navy with the last example eventually being converted to become the Royal Navy prototype
- 2 Trainer aircraft for a proposed RAF use.

LEFT Original artist's impressions of the final proposed WG-13 variants: Utility for the Army Air Corps, Civilian and French Army Attack Variants. *(AgustaWestland)*

This was indeed the most complex helicopter programme attempted thus far. To minimise the complexity, however, and attempt to keep costs down, the powerplant, transmission and rotor systems were to be common to all of the WG-13 variants.

Package deal

In October 1967 the British and French governments agreed proposals for a so-called 'package deal' (worth a reported £80 million) to undertake the production of a range of three helicopter designs – the twin-engined SA.330 (later to be named Puma), the single-engined SA.340 (later to become the SA.341 Gazelle) and the WG-13 – with the manufacturing and cost of all three being shared between the two countries. The formal agreement was duly signed on 2 April the following year by Pierre Messmer, Minister for the French Armed Forces and Sir Patrick Reilly, British Ambassador to France.

The two major European helicopter manufacturers – Sud-Aviation of France and Westland Helicopters Ltd of Britain – were asked to collaborate over the engineering and manufacture of the aircraft with the latter being nominated as the design leader for the WG-13 project. Twelve such aircraft were ordered to shoulder the burden of the planned 2,400-hour flight test programme. By way of political compensation for the recent cancellation of the British-engined Anglo-French Variable Geometry (VG) fighter aircraft project, the proposed option to fit French engines to the Aéronavale aircraft was dropped and the new Rolls-Royce BS.360-07 Gem adopted across all of the variants. The first engine bench ran in September 1969, initially developing a mere 700shp, but by the time the fourth WG-13 flew it had achieved the original planned 800shp.

Cancellations

In September 1969, the project ran into political difficulties when the French Army cancelled their order for 150 of the WG-13T Armed Reconnaissance 'gun-ship' variant on the grounds of cost. With France already heavily committed to seven other collaborative projects – notably Concorde – money was understandably tight. Coupled with this, doubts also began to grow over the future of the order for the French Navy's WG-13V variant and

ABOVE Another of the Sud-Aviation/ Westland Helicopters Ltd collaborations, which formed part of the package deal, the SA.340 would eventually develop into the SA.341 Gazelle and equip not only the Army Air Corps and Fleet Air Arm but the Royal Air Force too. *(AgustaWestland)*

inevitably concerns were raised over the share of the development costs that had been a key part of the original agreement.

To go some way in offsetting the cancellation costs – which equated to around 30% of the overall expenditure – additional work was later apportioned to Société Nationale Industrielle Aérospatiale (SNIAS – formed by a merger with the other French state-owned companies including Sud Aviation and Nord Aviation in 1970), including the design of the role-fit equipment for the UK aircraft and the folding tail boom and rear undercarriage sponsons for the Naval variants.

Design features

BELOW

WG-13T Armed Reconnaissance version with tail-dragger wheel arrangement, three-man crew, chin turret and missiles mounted on stub wings.

(AgustaWestland)

The WG-13 design represented a major departure from traditional helicopter manufacturing techniques. The extensive use of plastics for aerodynamic fairings and of printed circuitry for the aircraft's electrical systems were just some of the new technologies incorporated from the start.

The specification called for the aircraft to be small enough for air portability in Short Belfast and C-130 Hercules aircraft, a folded size not exceeding 34ft long, 12ft wide and 10ft 6in in height and had to fit on a carrier lift (54ft × 44ft) without folding the tail. The overall length was not to exceed 50ft.

With the cabin dimensions dictating a reasonably deep fuselage, minimising the height of anything above the roof became a major consideration. Up until now, the main rotor gearboxes fitted to the original Sikorsky designs built under licence by Westland – the Dragonfly, Whirlwind and Wessex – were several feet in height as a result of using conventional epicyclic gearing.

To achieve the necessary reduction from the engine input speed of 6,000rpm to a main rotor output of a mere 318rpm, a two-stage system incorporating a conventional spiral bevel gear stage and a new 'conformal' gear stage was proposed.

Westland had been the first company to use conformal gearing in helicopters, having begun a private-venture research programme as early as 1959. The shape of the conformal gearing teeth permitted the transfer of higher power with gears of lower dimensions and weights with improved lubrication properties and saved weight by using up to 40% fewer components and bearings than traditional gearing. This also allowed the main rotor gearbox to be of shallow,

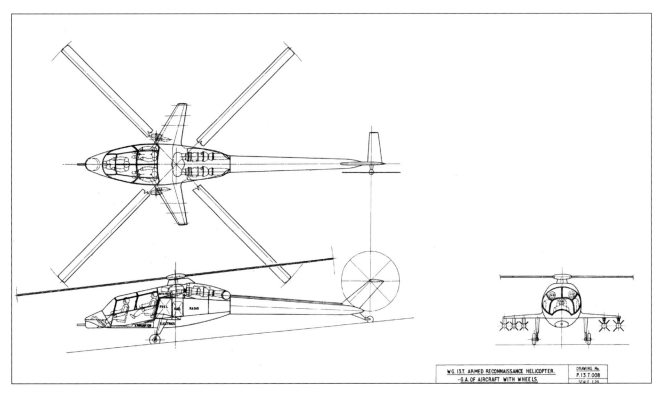

WG. 13.T. ARMED RECONNAISSANCE HELICOPTER.
-G.A. OF AIRCRAFT WITH WHEELS.

DRAWING No.
P. 13. T. 008
SCALE 1:20

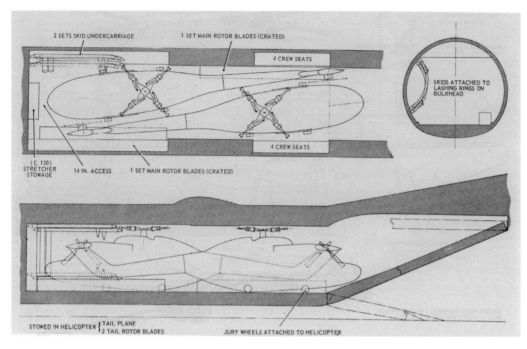

2 SETS SKID UNDERCARRIAGE
1 SET MAIN ROTOR BLADES (CRATED)
4 CREW SEATS
SKIDS ATTACHED TO LASHING RINGS ON BULKHEAD
4 CREW SEATS
(C 130) STRETCHER STOWAGE
14 IN. ACCESS
1 SET MAIN ROTOR BLADES (CRATED)
STOWED IN HELICOPTER { TAIL PLANE 2 TAIL ROTOR BLADES
JURY WHEELS ATTACHED TO HELICOPTER

LEFT One of the key design considerations was the ability to fit an aircraft into the cargo hold of a C-130 Hercules transport aircraft. *(AgustaWestland)*

squat construction while the positioning of the engines immediately aft of the transmission area meant that the desired lower overall height of the aircraft could be achieved. As well as making this ideal for air transportability of the Army variant to operational theatres, it also lent itself to the planned operation from small ships where hangar height was a prime issue.

Semi-rigid rotor trials

Understanding vibration – an ever-present problem with helicopters – and the general performance of the semi-rigid main rotor was addressed by fitting two Scout helicopters at Hayes with a scaled-down version of the proposed rotor head. Trials began with XP189 on 31 August 1970 and it was joined by XP191

BELOW XP189 – one of two specially modified Westland Scout AH.1s fitted with a scaled-down version of the rigid rotor head design intended for the WG-13. *(AgustaWestland)*

a year later. These rigid rotor trials would continue at RAE Bedford until October 1977.

While the rigid rotor had been flown successfully on the two Scout trials aircraft, the transmission system as a whole had not. To begin to test the system and determine its effect on the WG-13's structure, an airframe rotor spin rig – cruelly referred to by some as the 'Iron Chicken' – was installed in a special running pen at nearby RNAS Yeovilton during August 1970. Noise generated by the constant testing was less of an issue here than it was at the increasingly urbanised Yeovil. Built from components taken straight from the production line and including

a hut fitted out with a set of engine controls to replicate the intended cockpit design, the first rotor runs were carried out at Yeovilton on 24 September and allowed the test pilots to gain some familiarity with engine operations.

Choosing a name

The name for the new helicopter had to conform to three rules: it had to be bilingual; it had to be capable of being prefixed with the word 'Sea' for naval versions; and preferably it would begin with the letter 'W' to fit with Westland's tradition of naming their aircraft.

RIGHT The mock-up of the WG-13 under construction at Hayes. *(AgustaWestland)*

Their first suggestion, therefore, was 'Warrior'; 'Wildcat' was even put forward (a portent of things to come).

But the die was eventually cast when, during the summer of 1970, it was announced that in line with the naming of the other Anglo-French helicopter types after animals, the production WG-13 would be renamed as the 'Lynx' – a name put forward by no fewer than 17 Westland employees. Logically, it was proposed that the Naval variant would eventually become the 'Sea Lynx', but it was decided that the translation into French as 'Lynx du Mer' was perhaps too much of a mouthful.

By now, programme cost estimates had reached £25 million, with an additional £6 million for the BS.360 engine development alone.

US interest

With more than a slight twist of irony, Sikorsky began negotiations with Westland in 1970 with a view to licence-building 200 examples of the Lynx in the event of it becoming selected by the US Navy for their Light Airborne Multi-purpose System (LAMPS) small-ship utility helicopter programme for use from destroyers. General Electric were expected to have built the RS.360 engine under licence and although second WG-13 prototype XW836 was demonstrated to the US Navy in March 1973, the proposal never came to fruition.

RAF trainer variant

Another version that never saw the light of day was an HT Mk.1 training model for the Royal Air Force. Thirteen examples were proposed as replacements for the ageing Westland Whirlwind HAR Mk.10s being used by the Central Flying School. The requirement would eventually be cancelled in the defence cuts of 1975 before any aircraft had been built.

First flight

In overall bright yellow paint finish, the first prototype – XW835 – made its first of two short flights at Yeovil in the late afternoon of Sunday 21 March 1971. At the controls were Westland's Chief Test Pilot Ron Gellatly, together

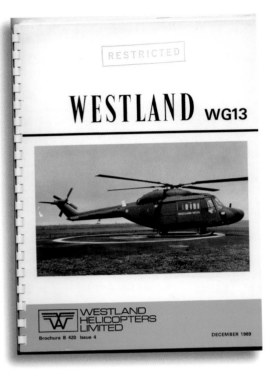

LEFT The WG-13 sales brochure dated December 1969 showing the mock-up at Hayes. *(AgustaWestland)*

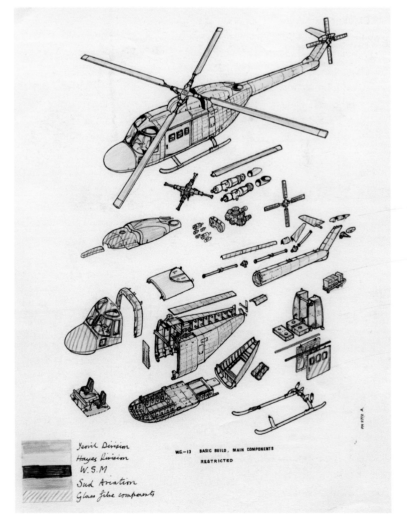

BELOW The break-down of sub-assemblies for the Basic variant of the WG-13 showing the share of work across the Westland and Sud Aviation factories. *(AgustaWestland)*

PROTOTYPES OF MANY COLOURS

Appropriately enough, the WG-13 programme benefitted from having no fewer than 13 prototype and pre-production aircraft to undertake various elements of the flight testing regime ahead of the production aircraft entering service. In order to help distinguish the first five basic prototypes from one another from a distance, each received its own individual, easily identifiable colour. The last of the prototype aircraft, XX911 – a Mk.4 for the French Navy – made its first flight on 18 September 1973.

The rationale for painting the prototype aircraft in a myriad of different colours has never been explained, but it did make for easier identification of the aircraft.

XW835 Yellow
XW836 Grey
XW837 Red
XW838 Blue
XW839 Orange

ABOVE The second to fifth WG-13 Basic and Utility prototypes – XW836, XW837, XW838 and XW839 – under construction at Yeovil. (AgustaWestland)

ABOVE First Basic prototype aircraft XW835 in overall yellow. (AgustaWestland)

BELOW XW835 and XW837 flying over the Westland Helicopters Ltd factory at Yeovil. (AgustaWestland)

ABOVE The pale blue fourth prototype, XW838. Note the rear-facing left-hand cockpit seat allowing the flight test engineer to operate instruments in the cabin. (AgustaWestland)

BELOW XW837 and XW838 are joined by the first Naval prototype WG-13, XX469, in the flight shed at Yeovil. (AgustaWestland)

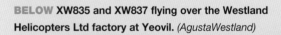

with Roy Moxam and Flight Test Observer David Gibbings. Ground running had taken a mere five days to complete and the aircraft had flown just eight months later than had been originally scheduled back in 1967.

XW835 was followed on 28 September by the third prototype aircraft, XW837. Individual unit costs were now reported as £220,000 for the basic Army version, rising to £275,000 for the more complex Naval variant.

Joining Moxam and fellow Westland Test Pilot Mike Ginn to undertake the test programme were former Fairey Test Pilots John Morton and Keith Chadbourn. Vibration issues plagued the early test programme and the prototypes had to have internal bracing fitted – even sections of industrial reinforced steel girders – in a bid to try to counter the problem.

PT6 engine

As the prototype flight test development programme got under way, problems with the new Bristol Siddeley BS.360 engine persisted with high oil consumption and compressor turbine overheating issues, which led to the prototypes being forced to operate at reduced power levels. Such were the issues that the first prototype had actually made its first flight with its engines limited to just 600shp. The fracture of an internal oil pipe, causing ignition of oil, which in turn led to weakening of a turbine wheel, had resulted in

the aircraft crashing near Martock on 22 December 1971.

The French, who from the start had never been keen to opt for the British engine, lobbied once again for the adoption of the United Aircraft of Canada PT6 as a contingency plan. Already well proven, use of the PT6 was seen as a way to potentially make the Lynx more attractive to a lucrative North American market and would possibly improve its chances of being selected for the LAMPS programme there. A three-month study was conducted in early 1972 that culminated in XW835 being re-engined with a pair of 750shp PT6B-34 engines using the same mounting and drive arrangements as the Gem but with noticeably different cowlings. In this configuration, the aircraft first flew on 19 July 1976 in the hands of Westland Test Pilot Keith Chadbourn, receiving the civil registration G-BEAD.

ABOVE The first Basic prototype XW835 thought to have been photographed during its maiden flight at Yeovil on 21 March 1971 ahead of the official launch to the press the following day. The aircraft is fitted with modified Wessex main rotor blades suitably cropped to length. *(Fred Ballam)*

BELOW XW835, registered as G-BEAD and fitted with Pratt & Whitney PT6B-34 engines. *(AgustaWestland)*

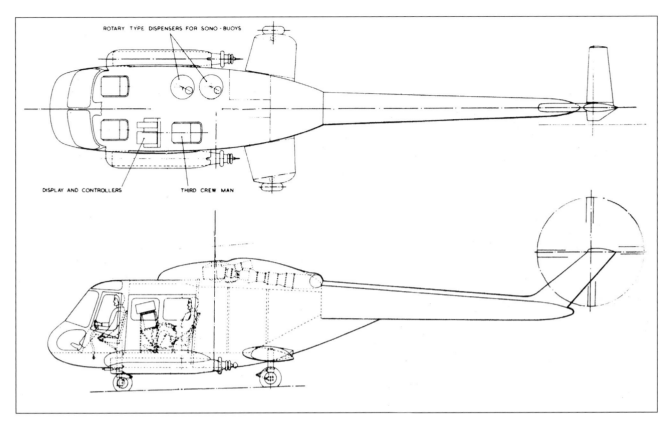

ROTARY TYPE DISPENSERS FOR SONO - BUOYS

DISPLAY AND CONTROLLERS

THIRD CREW MAN

ABOVE Almost there: schematic of the Naval variant of the WG-13 complete with sonar gear in the cabin. *(AgustaWestland)*

Sea Lynx

The sixth WG-13 to fly – XX469 – took to the skies over Yeovil on 25 May 1972. As the first of the pre-production aircraft completed to a Naval configuration, it featured the folding tail pylon required for small-ship operations and a tricycle-wheeled undercarriage (with main units housed in sponsons) and a castoring nosewheel.

Its involvement in the trials programme, however, was all too brief. It crashed at Yeovil on 21 November following the failure of a coupling in the tail rotor drive while in the hover and was written off. The crew, former Fairey

RIGHT Display model of the original WG-13 Naval variant with blunt nose. *(AgustaWestland)*

Test Pilot John Morton and Flight Test Engineer Peter Wilson-Chalon, were lucky to escape with only minor injuries. It would not be until the second Navalised pre-production aircraft, XX510, flew on 6 March 1973 in the hands of Keith Chadbourn and Bob Clarke, that the Naval variant trials could resume.

ABOVE LEFT The bearded figure of Westland's Deputy Chief Test Pilot, John Morton in Lynx prototype XX469. A former RN Pilot, Morton had joined Westlands from Fairey where he had been one of the test pilots for the Fairey Rotodyne project. *(AgustaWestland)*

ABOVE John Morton at the controls of XX469. *(AgustaWestland)*

RIGHT XX469 undergoing landing trials using the rolling platform at NAD RAE Bedford to simulate the moving deck of a small ship. *(AgustaWestland)*

BELOW A brochure on the Naval Lynx variant produced by Westland. *(AgustaWestland)*

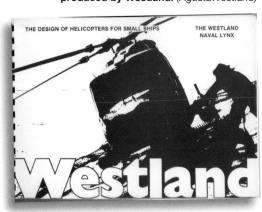

RIGHT Navalised prototype Lynx XX510 carrying out deck landing trials aboard the Leander-class frigate HMS *Sirius*. Note how small and confined the flight deck is. *(AgustaWestland)*

Into service

No. 700L Naval Air Squadron formed at RNAS Yeovilton on 1 September 1976 and was officially commissioned two weeks later on 16 September as the Intensive Flying Trials Unit (IFTU) for the Lynx HAS Mk.2 under the command of Lt Cdr Geoff Cavalier, RN. Initially with just one aircraft, XZ229, the unit was in fact the first ever Anglo-Dutch unit, receiving its first of two UH-14A Lynx aircraft for the Royal Netherlands Navy in October 1976. These aircraft had also been procured to replace their Wasps. By March the following year the squadron had eight aircraft on charge, reducing to six when the two Dutch examples left for their native homeland in May.

United Kingdom Westland Lynx variants

Lynx AH Mk.1

The AH Mk.1 was the Utility version for the Army Air Corps ordered to Specification 269 D&P Issue 2. Fitted with skidded undercarriage, it had an AUM of 9,600lb making it the lightest

Commissioning Order

BY JOHN OLIVER ROBERTS, *Companion of the Most Honourable Order of the Bath, Rear Admiral in Her Majesty's Fleet and Flag Officer Naval Air Command.*

A511/2/2

The Admiralty Board of the Defence Council having directed that number 700L Naval Air Squadron is to be commissioned in Her Majesty's Ship HERON on Wednesday 1st September 1976, or as soon afterwards as circumstances permit, you are to proceed to commission that Squadron accordingly and to cause the utmost despatch to be used, so far as the same may depend on you, in preparing for flying operations.

Number 700L Squadron will be administered by me, and all matters concerning defects, omissions, etcetera, bearing on the satisfactory completion of preparation for your task are to be reported in accordance with current regulations.

Given under my hand in Her Majesty's Ship HERON this thirty-first day of August 1976.

J. O. Roberts

REAR ADMIRAL

To :- Lieutenant Commander G. A. Cavalier, Royal Navy

Copies to :-

The Deputy Under Secretary of State (Navy)
The Commanding Officer, HMS HERON

LEFT The Commissioning Order for 700L Naval Air Squadron which formed at RNAS Yeovilton on 1 September 1976 under the command of Lieutenant Commander Geoff Cavalier, RN. *(FAAM)*

of all of the variants. Its role was to provide support to battlefield tactical activity through troop deployment, casualty evacuation and equipment supply and resupply.

Powered by a pair of 900shp Gem 2 engines, the first flight took place on 1 June 1977. The inclusion of the Tube-launched,

Optically-tracker, Wire-guided (TOW) missile system capability during the early 1980s saw the AH Mk.1 take on the anti-tank capability, making the aircraft a formidable aerial asset on the battlefield. Production of the AH Mk.1 reached 113 aircraft before being superseded by the much-improved AH Mk.7 in 1984.

ABOVE Lynx AH Mk.1 XZ179 firing a TOW missile during training. *(AgustaWestland)*

THE FIRST RECORD BREAKER – XX153

Fast and agile, the Lynx was a prime contender for an attempt at the world airspeed record for a helicopter. The first Lynx to break a world record was XX153, flown by Roy Moxam and Flight Test Engineer Michael Ball on 20 June 1972. Flying at a height of just 300ft over a straight-line course near Glastonbury, the aircraft achieved a speed of 200mph (321.7km/h). Two days later the same aircraft and crew achieved 197.9mph (318.5km/h) over a closed-circuit course in south Somerset at 600ft.

RIGHT Lynx Utility prototype XX153 demonstrates its manoeuvrability by being rolled by Roy Moxam, an achievement made possible by virtue of the semi-rigid rotor head. *(AgustaWestland)*

ABOVE Lynx ZD560 was originally built as a AH Mk.5 before being converted to basic AH Mk.7 standard. It spent its entire service life at Boscombe Down as a trials airframe.

Lynx AH Mk.5

Ahead of the start of production of the AH Mk.7 as the much-improved successor to the AH Mk.1, a batch of three aircraft was ordered as interim variants in order to conduct trials with the MoD Procurement Executive fleet: ZD285, ZD559 and ZD560. The following batch of eight aircraft were also expected to be to AH Mk.5 standard, but only the first two – ZE375 and ZE376 – emerged as such, with the remaining six aircraft coming off the production line as the first of the production AH Mk.7s.

Powered by Gem 42 engines and with an AUM of 10,000lb, the first of the AH Mk.5 aircraft was delivered to RAE Farnborough on 30 November 1984 with the second being flown to RAE Bedford on 26 February the following year.

Lynx AH Mk.7

In the late 1980s and through the 1990s, the AH Mk.1 version was progressively converted to the improved and strengthened AH Mk.7 configuration to Specification B2022, Issue 2. The conversion programme was carried out at RNAY Fleetlands, Gosport, and eventually saw all but eight of the Mk.1 fleet converted, which consisted of the retrofitting of a new three-pinion main rotor gearbox, cooling modifications, new hydraulic pumps, armoured crew seats and the provision for Infrared Countermeasures (IRCM) engine exhaust ducts to help dissipate exhaust gases and thereby reduce the aircraft's thermal signature.

Strengthening of the tailcone also allowed for the fitting of a reverse-direction tail rotor that helped to resolve a lack of tail rotor authority in the hover. Composite tail rotor blades were also fitted. At 7ft 9in in diameter, the tail rotor was 6in greater than the original metal-bladed version on the AH Mk.1.

As a result of the very high usage rate of Lynx metal main rotor blades during Operation Granby (the British military operations during the 1991 Gulf War), the embodiment of composite main rotor blades (CMRBs), as already fitted to the AH Mk.9, was brought forward to June 1992 and the aircraft's AUM increased to 10,750lb.

A batch of 15 new-build AH Mk.7s were produced at Yeovil with the first making its initial flight there on 7 November 1985. Deliveries to the AAC began on 7 July 1986.

The AH Mk.7 was finally retired from service during the summer of 2015 with the aircraft being inducted into the Wildcat Donor Programme at AAC Middle Wallop. One example, XZ194, was officially gifted to the IWM at Duxford and another, XZ675, to the Museum of Army Flying at Middle Wallop where it joined the original Army prototype XX153 on display.

LEFT Although sporting Army titles, Lynx AH Mk.7, XZ205, seen here, was in use with the Royal Marines of 847 NAS who also operated the type. *(Crown Copyright/ LA(Phot) Billy Bunting)*

BELOW Lynx ZG887, one of the new-build AH Mk.9 aircraft, conducting UN peacekeeping operations with the AAC in Bosnia during the 1990s. *(AgustaWestland)*

The rest have been reduced to spares and sold as scrap or to private individuals.

Lynx AH Mk.9

Designed to Specification B2593, Issue 2 (dated August 1989) for a Light Utility Helicopter (LUH), the AH Mk.9 variant saw the aircraft's AUM increased to 11,300lb.

However, for the aircraft to be able to withstand this increase in weight, the original skidded undercarriage had to be replaced with a lightweight, wheeled undercarriage.

Only those aircraft that had been built from the outset as AH Mk.7s (with the strengthened lower fuselage) were capable of being modified, meaning that the earlier AH Mk.1 to AH Mk.7 airframes were ruled out.

The metal main rotor blades were replaced with composite British Experimental Rotor Programme (BERP) versions and secure speech radio and GEC AD 2780 TACAN were fitted. As a Utility variant, with Tactical Troop Transport, Logistic Support, CASEVAC, Airborne Command Post primary roles and a secondary Liaison role, all TOW missile and stores provisions were removed.

The prototype AH Mk.9 first flew in 1989. As well as the eight conversions from AH Mk.7, a batch of 16 new-build AH Mk.9 aircraft were also ordered with the first, ZG884, making its maiden flight on 20 July 1990. All but one (which had been written off in an accident) of these aircraft would later be converted to AH Mk.9A standard.

Lynx AH Mk.9A

Performance issues with the Gem-powered Lynx AH Mk.7 were first highlighted during the 2003 Iraq War where aircraft had been fitted with sand filters, IRCM exhaust ducts, armoured seats, defensive aid suites and TOW missiles. Conceived during the Cold War and expected to operate in much cooler European climes, the high ambient temperatures experienced in the

BELOW Lynx AH Mk.9A, ZG914, fitted with the LHTEC CTS-400N engine.

Lynx 3

In 1982, Westland unveiled proposals for what was termed the Lynx 3. The aircraft was designed with the extended and much deeper-in cross-section tailcone from the company's WG-30 helicopter.

This was followed, in late 1983, by the 1,260shp Gem 60-powered Naval Lynx 3 for the Royal Australian Navy. Differing from the Army variant in having a wheeled undercarriage, the aircraft was 29in longer than a Lynx HAS Mk.3 and also featured the Ferranti *Seaspray 3* 360-degree radar in a ventral-mounted radome under the nose, a dorsal-mounted night vision turret, dunking sonar, sonobuoys, towed magnetic anomaly detector (MAD), *Orange Crop* ESM, BERP rotor blades and was armed with *Sea Skua* and/or Marconi *Stingray* homing torpedoes.

The Australian order never materialised, however, and the aircraft never went into production. Only one aircraft, ZE477, was ever completed as a demonstrator.

Westland 606

In a private venture by Westland aimed at breaking into the American executive helicopter market, the proposed Westland 606 saw the basic WG-13 airframe stretched by 12in ahead of the main rotor gearbox, while the cabin was fitted with leather-upholstered seats and configured to be capable of carrying between 7 and 12 passengers. Two versions were envisaged: the 606-10 with Pratt & Whitney PT6-34B engines and the 606-20 with a pair of Gems. The first flight of a prototype aircraft was scheduled for December 1975.

Although the fuselage of the now-retired XW836 was converted to become the 606 mock-up in the summer of 1974 and statically displayed as such at both the SBAC Show, Farnborough, that year and the Helicopter Association of America at Anaheim, California, ultimately no interest was shown in the design and the 606 was cancelled before any examples were built. In its place, the company forged ahead with their Westland WG-30, which used many of the transmission components from the Lynx with a larger fuselage. Although 41 examples were built, it was not a commercial success and was also eventually cancelled.

RIGHT ZE477, the sole Lynx 3 battlefield helicopter prototype of 13,000lb and a top speed of 160 knots. *(AgustaWestland)*

BELOW The Westland 606 mock-up at Yeovil in 1974 showing the longer fuselage. *(AgustaWestland)*

LEFT The leather-upholstered cockpit of the Westland 606 mock-up. *(AgustaWestland)*

BELOW Executive seating for up to 12 people in the enlarged cabin of the Westland 606. *(AgustaWestland)*

Middle East combined with this increase in AUM led to the aircraft being flown with no power reserves. This left it vulnerable and unable to conduct some daytime operations.

A similar situation presented itself three years later when the aircraft were first deployed to Afghanistan, this time the problem being further compounded by the thinner air found at the high operating altitudes. As a result, the AH Mk.7 was limited to operations during the Afghan winter months only.

As the British commitment in Afghanistan increased, an urgent operating requirement (UOR) was formulated to properly address the situation. Existing Gem-powered AH Mk.9 aircraft were re-engined with two much more capable LHTEC CTS800-4N powerplants. With a normal operating crew of three, the AH Mk.9A can carry up to four passengers and conduct convoy overwatch, support helicopter escort, reconnaissance and surveillance and the movement of personnel.

The conversion work was carried out at AgustaWestland, Yeovil, with the first example, ZG889, making its initial flight there in September 2009, just 11 months after the award of the contract. The new variant was airfreighted to Afghanistan in April 2010 and entered operational service there with 9 Regiment AAC on 1 May.

Royal Navy variants
Lynx HAS Mk.2
The first RN variant of the Lynx was the HAS Mk.2. Powered by a pair of 900shp Gem 2 engines and resplendent in overall Oxford Blue paint scheme, the aircraft entered operational service with HMS *Birmingham* in 1977.

Lynx HAS Mk.3
Specification 1246, Issue 2 (dated October 1981) detailed the requirement for upgrading the Lynx HAS Mk.2 to have an AUM of 10,500lb and be fitted with uprated Gem Mk.201 engines.

Beginning in June 1984, all remaining HAS Mk.2 aircraft (with the exception of XZ236) were converted to HAS Mk.3 standard by the Naval Aircraft Support Unit (NASU) at RNAS Yeovilton. Completion took place in 1988. A batch of 20 new-build aircraft were produced at Yeovil (ZD249 to ZD268) between 1982 and 1983, followed by a further three (ZD565 to ZD567) in 1985 as attrition replacements for the aircraft lost during Operation Corporate (the 1982 British operation to retake the Falkland Islands from invading Argentine forces). The converted aircraft were retrofitted with the Gem 41-1 Mk.204 engines producing 1,120shp each and all were fitted with MIR-2 *Orange Crop* electronic support measures (ESM)

RIGHT Lynx HAS Mk.2, XZ723 '753' of 815 NAS HQ Flight, in the original Oxford Blue scheme, landing on the deck of HMS *Sheffield*, June 1981.
(Chris Wood)

equipment and the capability of carrying the Ericsson AN/ALQ-167(V) *Yellow Veil* electronic countermeasures (ECM) pods and BAe *Sea Skua* anti-shipping missile.

Lynx HAS Mk.3ICE

A total of five Lynx HAS Mk.3s (XZ233, XZ235, XZ238, XZ241 and XZ246) were converted by NASU (later AMG) at RNAS Yeovilton, the Naval Aircraft Trials Installation Unit (NATIU) at RNAS Lee-on-Solent and by RNAY Fleetlands between 1986 and 1997. Vertically mounted Zeiss Survey Camera pod or Leica cameras could be fitted for survey work carried out in conjunction with the British Antarctic Survey team, for whom the Lynx provided a great deal of assistance over the years.

Unencumbered by armament (as a prerequisite of operating in the Antarctic) and therefore very much lighter than its more warlike siblings, the HAS Mk.3ICE variant was generally considered to be the sportiest of all marks of Lynx.

Of the aircraft converted, XZ241 was lost in a non-fatal crash in Antarctica in February 2004 and, following the near loss of HMS *Endurance* in the Antarctic in 2008, the final two aircraft were relegated to training roles. XZ238 made the last flight of a HAS Mk.3ICE when it was flown to the Wildcat Donor and Strip for Spares Programme at Middle Wallop on 24 January 2013.

Lynx HAS Mk.3S

With the original Naval Staff Target (NST 6679) proposal for a full upgrade of the HAS Mk.3 – to which was originally allocated the designation HAS Mk.8 – having been rejected by the MoD, plans were instead put in place to gradually phase in the Central Tactical System (CTS) (NSR 6117), integrated 360-degree radar (NSR 6637) and Passive Identification Device (PID) modifications (NSR 6643), in order to improve operational capability.

Phase 1 of the subsequent conversion programme began with the introduction of the

ABOVE The last Lynx HAS Mk.3ICE to fly: XZ238 departing RNAS Yeovilton on 24 January 2013.

BELOW The busy 702 NAS flightline at RNAS Yeovilton with a number of Lynx HAS Mk.3GMS. No. 702 NAS decommissioned in August 2014, passing its training role to 815 NAS.

RIGHT A Lynx HAS Mk.3GMS of 829 NAS HQ Flight, RNAS Portland, fitted with a AN/ALQ-167(V) *Yellow Veil* ECM pod, GEC *Sandpiper* FLIR, Loral *Challenger* IRCM 'lanterns' as well as Tracor M130 Chaff/ Flare dispensers just forward of the tailcone. *(via David Elford)*

GEC Marconi AD3400 and PTR377 secure speech radios and Racal *Orange Crop* ESM. The last seven production Lynx for the Royal Navy (ZF557 to ZF563) were completed as HAS Mk.3S straight off the production line with ZF557 making its first flight from Yeovil on 12 October 1987 and the last aircraft being delivered in 1988.

Lynx HAS Mk.3GM and Mk.3GMS

With Lynx being deployed to support the Armilla Patrol in the Persian Gulf, it was deemed necessary to upgrade the aircraft with sand filters for the engine air intakes and to modify the gearboxes for operation in hot ambient conditions. This led to two new standards of Mk.3: the HAS Mk.3GM ('Gulf Mod') or Mk.3 GMS ('Gulf Mod, Secure Speech').

Deployed aircraft were also capable of being fitted with the Ericsson Radar Electronics AN/ ALQ-167(V) D- to J-band anti-shipping missile ESM pod.

During the Gulf War of 1990–91, the Lynx were also augmented with GEC *Sandpiper* FLIR

LEFT The heavy machine-gun pod (HMP) fitted on the starboard weapon carrier, together with ALQ-147 IR jammer, as installed on aircraft deployed on the Armilla Patrol during the late 1980s. *(via David Elford)*

fitted to the port weapons carrier, Tracor M130 chaff and flare dispensers and a pair of Loral *Challenger* IRCM jamming pods mounted above the cockpit. The appearance of the latter led to them receiving the nickname 'lanterns'. A 0.5in helicopter machine-gun pod (HMP) could also be fitted to the weapon carriers.

Lynx HAS Mk.3CTS

Phase 2 of the HAS Mk.3 upgrade involved the introduction of the Central Tactical System (CTS) developed jointly between Westland and Racal, from whose Racal Avionics Management System (RAMS) 4000 it was derived.

The modification included the installation of a 14in Tactical Situation Display (TSD) colour cathode ray tube screen in the centre of the instrument panel for targeting, a Data Transfer Device (DTD) in the interseat console to allow tactical information to be uploaded from a planning computer via a cartridge into the CTS itself and two Control and Display Navigation Units (CDNUs). The CTS could then be used to control the weapon settings, radios, navigation functions, ESM, *Sea Owl* PID, MAD and some of the radar functions.

Externally, the aircraft were easily identifiable by the addition of two forward flotation bags stowed in compartments on either side of the cockpit beneath the footwell windows.

XZ236, the only aircraft not to have already been converted from HAS Mk.2, was the first to undergo modification to HAS Mk.3CTS at Yeovil, making its maiden first flight from there on 25 January 1989 in the hands of Westland Test Pilot Mike Fuller. One HAS Mk.3 – XZ697 – was also converted, followed by the five HAS Mk.3S production aircraft ZF557, ZF558, ZF560, ZF562 and ZF563. These six aircraft were delivered to RNAS Portland: three to once again form 700L NAS – this time as the Lynx Operational Flight Trials Unit (LOFTU), officially commissioned on 6 July 1990 – and the remainder embarked in HMS *Avenger*, *Ambuscade* and *Amazon*.

Lynx HMA Mk.8

Phase 3 was the conversion of the Lynx HAS Mk.3 to HAS Mk.8. The selection of a contractor to provide radar having becoming complicated, approvals were instead given to

LYNX HAS MK.3 SUB-VARIANTS	
HAS.3S	Aircraft modified with secure speech radio and associated wiring looms
HAS.3SGM	Aircraft modified to 'Gulf Mod' standard (sand filter mods, gearbox mods, etc.) with secure speech
HAS.3CTS	Modified with CTS – an interim conversion between HAS.3SGM and HMA.8. All eight aircraft thus modified were subsequently reworked to HMA.8 standard
HAS.3ICE	Specially modified aircraft (high-vis red scheme, camera fit, change of cabin fire extinguisher position to prevent fouling by internal loads) for use by *Endurance* Flight.

proceed with the PID element in a way that would allow the provision of all radar choices including a repositioned *Seaspray* unit. This short-term development configuration eventually became the ultimate production standard when the requirement for 360-degree radar was eventually cancelled on cost grounds.

To undertake the development of the various elements of the programme, three aircraft were nominated: ZD266 would become the CTS development aircraft, while ZD267 and XZ236 would carry out airframe and avionic development respectively.

As with most projects of this nature, the late addition of further requirements only served to increase its complexity. An increased AUM from 4,875kg to 5,330kg and the introduction of composite main rotor blades and enhanced sensor systems meant that there were now four distinct phases to the programme.

In June 1992 an initial contract, worth £20 million, was placed with Westland for the supply of an initial 25 modification kits to convert the HAS Mk.3 to HAS Mk.8. Stress analysis revealed areas that required uprating and strengthening in order to absorb the increase in the aircraft's weight.

The entire nose structure forward of the windscreen was removed and replaced with a new 'stepped' version to allow the fitting of the GEC Sensors *Sea Owl* PID turret and the hyperbolic radar scanner beneath. Despite having a 360-degree radome, the aircraft was initially fitted with the 180-degree Ferranti *Seaspray* Mk.1 radar, owing to cost constraints. This meant that the aircraft could not fly away from a target during a *Sea Skua* attack until the

LYNX HMA MK.8 FLEETS WITHIN FLEETS

The progressive upgrading of the HMA Mk.8 fleet spawned a series of sub-variant designations that allowed fleet planners to properly determine status and capability while the modification programmes were being carried out:

HMA.8	Original standard of conversion, carried out at Westlands, Yeovil, and RNAY/NARO/DARA Fleetlands. All aircraft subsequently upgraded to DSP (Digital Signal Processor) standard
HMA.8DSP	HMA.8 retrofitted with DSP (identifiable as being aircraft with an aerial box halfway along the tail rotor driveshaft fairings)
HMA.8SRU	SATURN radio upgrade. Second-generation anti-jam tactical UHF radios for NATO. Modified at Mann Aviation Group Engineering, Fairoaks, starting in 2007.

missile had hit the target. Not very comforting for the crew! The original metal 'gullwing' doors were also replaced by larger, reshaped composite doors.

Major strengthening work was undertaken to absorb the forces created by the reverse-direction tail rotor which gave better yaw control over the HAS Mk.3, enabling it to hover in 40-knot crosswinds even at maximum AUM. Both sides of the rear fuselage had the aluminium skins replaced by increased-gauge material and doubler plates installed. The tailcone was completely rebuilt using thicker-gauge material and incorporated additional stringers and doubler plates.

The first 13 aircraft were converted by Westland themselves at Yeovil, beginning in June 1993. Thereafter, the 25 remaining aircraft were converted by the RNAY (later Defence Aviation Repair Agency) at Fleetlands. Although nine more kits were still available, the programme was suspended by January 2002 and the final conversion aircraft, XZ725, made its first flight from there on 14 May that year.

The final development for the HMA Mk.8 was a combined modifications package which was undertaken by Mann Aviation Group Engineering (MAGE) at Fairoaks. This was an upgrade to the existing SATURN radio unit (SRU)-configured aircraft and saw the introduction of improved lighting, successor identification friend or foe (SIFF), airborne solid-state recorder, cockpit voice recorder and the introduction of night vision goggle-compatible cockpit. This substantial programme finally concluded in March 2010.

Displaying the Lynx

As a fast, agile helicopter, it was natural to want to put the aircraft through its paces in front of the public. Between 1978 and 1980, 702 NAS entered the Lynx HAS Mk.2 into the British Helicopter Championships with notable successes.

From 1992, 702 NAS displayed their HAS Mk.3s under the name 'Lynx Pairs', changing to 'The Lynx Pair' in 2000. In 2004, however, the 'Pair' became 'The Black Cats': a name inspired by the squadron's badge and also the naval slang term of 'black catting' (a form of one-upmanship, having done or owned something better than someone else).

From 2007 the team replaced one of its HAS Mk.3 aircraft with a HMA Mk.8 and both received a special paint scheme. With the retirement of the HAS Mk.3 fleet, the team changed over to two HMA Mk.8s; then, in its final year under 702 NAS parentage, one Lynx was replaced by a Wildcat HMA.2 of 825 NAS before the Lynx was finally withdrawn from the team in 2015.

Aircraft losses

Three HMA Mk.8 aircraft were unfortunately lost in accidents. The first, XZ728 of 210 Flight, was washed off the flight deck of HMS Monmouth by a freak wave in February 1997, just weeks after emerging from conversion to HMA Mk.8. Quickly salvaged but deemed to be beyond economic repair due to salt water damage, she was later restored and placed on display at the RNAS Yeovilton gate.

Sadly the second aircraft to crash also claimed the lives of the Pilot and Observer. Lieutenant Commander Rod Skidmore, RN, and Lieutenant Jenny Lewis, RN, of 227 Flight embarked in HMS Richmond were conducting live Sea Skua firings off the coast of Virginia, USA, on 12 June 2002 when their aircraft, XZ256, suffered a catastrophic engine failure. The intense fire that broke out quickly spread through to the second engine and the aircraft ditched into the sea. Although the naval photographer who had been seated in the cabin to photograph the missile firings managed to escape, the front crew were sadly not so lucky. The wreckage of the helicopter was eventually located and recovered from a depth of over 2 miles – the deepest underwater aircraft salvage operation ever undertaken by the Ministry of Defence – to allow investigators to pinpoint the cause of the crash.

The third HMA Mk.8 aircraft to be lost, XZ695 of 228 Flight HMS *Nottingham*, was forced to ditch in the Indian Ocean after running out of fuel in March 2005 and subsequently sank. Luckily the crew managed to make their escape.

BELOW A shot taken from the Observer's position of one aircraft during the Black Cats' 'carousel' manoeuvre at the RAF Waddington Air Show. *(Mike Curd)*

WESTLAND WG-13 PROTOTYPES AND LYNX PRODUCTION FOR BRITISH ARMED FORCES

WG-13 Lynx	5	XW835–XW839
	2	XX153 and XX907
	4	XX469, XX510, XX910 and XZ166
	2	XX904 and XX911 (French Navy)
Lynx AH Mk.1	113	XZ170–XZ199; XZ203–XZ222; XZ605–XZ617; XZ640–XZ655; XZ661–XZ681; ZD272–ZD284
Lynx HAS Mk.2	61	XZ227–XZ257; XZ689–XZ700; XZ719–XZ736
Lynx HAS Mk.3	30	ZD249–ZD268; ZD565–ZD567; ZF557–ZF563
Lynx AH Mk.5	5	ZD285; ZD559–ZD560; ZE375–ZE376
Lynx AH Mk.7	10	ZE377–ZE382; ZF537–ZF540
Lynx AH Mk.9	16	ZG884–ZG889; ZG914–ZG923
TOTAL	248	

Chapter Three

Anatomy of the Lynx HMA Mk.8

At exactly 50ft in length with rotors in the spread position, the Westland Lynx HMA Mk.8 is, in helicopter terms, relatively small. But its size is also its strength, making it capable of operating from many landing sites and vessels that larger aircraft are simply unable to. It is extremely versatile and, with a range of weapon systems and a highly effective radar, it can also pack a significant punch.

OPPOSITE The most obvious difference between the HAS Mk.3GMS and the HMA Mk.8 is the completely redesigned nose section forward of the windscreens, repositioning the radar scanner and ESM aerials and adding the PID turret.

ABOVE The starboard side of the nose with composite gullwing door open to reveal the equipment bay. The Pilot's footwell window has been removed for access.

RIGHT The Pilot's cockpit door in the latched-open position. Below the opening is the footstep.

RIGHT The outside air temperature gauge installed in the Observer's cockpit door window.

Although many of the panels and fairings were designed from the outset to be manufactured from composite materials – and indeed many previously metal ones have been replaced over the years – the Lynx is still very much of traditional construction.

Fuselage

The Lynx HMA Mk.8 structure comprises eight major component areas: the forward fuselage including the nose and cockpit, the lower fuselage, the cabin roof, the cabin doors, the engine and transmission fairings, the rear fuselage, the sponsons and the tail unit.

Nose

The most noticeable external difference between the earlier HAS Mk.2 and HAS Mk.3 versions and the later HMA Mk.8 is the completely redesigned nose section forward of the cockpit windows. This assembly, divided down the centreline into two halves by a vertical web, comprises forward equipment compartments accessible via hinged panels that are universally known as a result of their curvature as 'gullwing doors'. It is the mounting platform for the dorsal-mounted *Sea Owl* PID turret and the ventral-mounted radar scanner and its protective radome, and it also houses the radar cooling equipment as well as being the support structure for the ESM aerials.

Cockpit

Access to the cockpit is via hinged doors fitted on both sides: the Pilot from the right-hand side and the Observer from the left. Both doors have built-in pivoted latch arm assemblies that automatically extend as the doors open and engage with spring-loaded catches on the fuselage to enable them to be held in place. As the catches are released and the doors are closed, so the latch arms retract flush with the door structure again.

Both doors have fixed lower Perspex panels with the Observer's panel drilled to allow the fitting of an outside air temperature probe and gauge. The upper half of the doors have a fixed rear Perspex panel and a forward panel which can slide fully open on rails.

A small footstep is built into the side of the cockpit's outer structure and a short tubular

ABOVE The Observer's cockpit footstep with navigation light.

BELOW The blue filler cap for replenishing the windscreen washer bottle fitted in the nose.

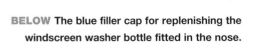

1 When the cockpit door is opened, a spring-loaded plunger operates a catch normally held flush in a slot on the outside of the door frame.

2 As the door opens further, so the catch extends fully …

3 … before engaging with a spigot on the outside of the nose to hold the door in place.

4 The catch is released by pushing the small tab at the outboard end of the plunger assembly. As the door closes, so the inboard end of the plunger comes into contact with the door frame and the catch is retracted back into its slot.

LEFT The windscreen wipers in their parked positions.

LEFT The bottles containing washer fluid for both the windscreen and the PID turret are situated behind the fairing (removed here) aft of the PID turret.

grab handle is fitted to the upper forward corner of the door aperture to help the crew when climbing in and out.

There are six main glazings in the cockpit. Two double-curvature front windscreens made from laminates of glass and plastic with an electrically heated transparent metal layer are designed to withstand the impact of small birds – an ever-present danger when operating at sea. The windscreens each have a motorised wiper blade operated by a rotary switch on the cockpit interseat console. The wiper blades have integral spray bars through which washer fluid, fed by an electric pump from a tank in the nose of the aircraft, can be sprayed.

Two overhead Perspex transparent panels are tinted to reduce glare, while Perspex footwell windows on either side of the cockpit beside the Pilot and Observer's feet allow the crew to see downwards. Unlike the others, these latter two panels can be removed to gain access to cockpit components, such as the heating ducting, by undoing quick-release fasteners.

Crew seats

The cockpit has a seat for the Pilot on the right-hand side and Observer on the left. There are two types of front seat that can be fitted, depending on the aircraft's role: a non-armoured seat for most day-to-day operations and an armoured seat for when the aircraft is likely to be flying in areas where the threat of being fired upon by small-arms weapons is high.

The seats can be adjusted for height using a lever at the front and are fitted with a standard five-point inertia-reel harness with quick-release fitting.

Mounted on the rear of the Pilot's and Observer's seats are first-aid kit pouches held in position by webbing straps and quick-release press studs. On the rear of the Pilot's seat is a small hand-held fire BCF (bromochlorodifluoromethane) extinguisher designed for use on most types of fire. It is mounted in a specially designed aluminium bracket that is screwed on to the rear of the seat and can be reached by either of the front crew in an emergency. The metal clasp that holds the bottle in place is secured by copper locking wire which can be broken easily by flipping open the catch; a broken piece of locking wire also serves as a tell-tale indicator that the bottle may have been removed from its stowage and may need inspection. Similarly,

RIGHT A standard, non-armoured Pilot's seat, minus cushion and Personal Survival Pack (PSP).

FAR RIGHT A number of extremely heavy Kevlar armour-protected front crew seats.

an indicator pin protruding from the top of the bottle's neck shows that the extinguisher is unserviceable and needs to be replaced.

Immediately aft of the seats is the control frame that runs from the floor on one side, up the side of the cockpit, across the roof and back down to the floor on the other side. Made from aluminium alloy components, this frame is effectively a hollow box that allows some of the flying control rods to run through it.

Instrument panels and cockpit lighting

The aircraft's instruments, indicators and switches are contained within a series of instrument panels and consoles mounted

on rubber anti-vibration shock absorbers immediately below the windscreen.

All of the cockpit instruments and panels feature integral lighting with the exception of the Outside Air Temperature (OAT) gauge and

FAR LEFT Details of the Observer's non-armoured seat with PSP, sheepskin cover and five-point harness. The connector at the side is to secure the PSP to the occupant. Just visible is the seat-height adjustment lever in the stowed (hinged-down) position.

LEFT The rear of the Pilot's seat, showing the inertia reel for the five-point harness, the hand-held fire extinguisher in its bracket and the first-aid kit.

BELOW The Lynx HMA Mk.8 cockpit in standard radar configuration.

the standby compass. A utility light can be mounted on either of two brackets positioned each side of the engine control quadrant. These can also be detached and used as hand-held lights if required. The lights can be focused and either red or white light can be selected using a rotating bezel ring.

When using Night Vision Goggles (NVGs), the cockpit is illuminated using five dimmable Electro-Luminescent Panels (ELPs) which cast an eerie pale green light over the instrument panels. Other instruments, such as the attention-getters and Centralised Warning Panel (CWP), are fitted with special Night Vision Device (NVD) filters to ensure that their light output does not interfere with the crew's night vision.

Pilot's instrument panel

The Pilot's instrument panel is situated on the right-hand side of the cockpit and contains the primary flight instruments: the combined torque indicator, attitude indicator (artificial horizon), radar altimeter, barometric altimeter (showing the aircraft's altitude), vertical speed indicator (showing the rate of climb or descent), heading indictor and standby artificial horizon.

The barometric instruments – barometric

TOP The cockpit instrument panels lit by conventional lighting …

ABOVE … and by Electro-Luminescent Panels for operations using Night Vision Devices.

RIGHT The Pilot's instrument panel.

1   Red attention-getter and cancel button
2   Amber attention-getter and cancel button
3   Red attention-getter and test button
4   Harpoon engaged light
5   Airspeed indicator
6   Attitude indicator
7   Radar altimeter
8   Torquemeter
9   Heading indicator
10 Barometric altimeter
11 Jettison mode selector
12 Standby attitude indicator
13 Vertical speed indicator
14 Ice accretion Vernier light control.

altimeters, airspeed indicators and vertical speed indicators – are all fed by the aircraft's pitot-static system. A stainless steel, electrically heated pitot head is fitted under the nose directly in front of the radome and directs airflow through a small hole in the middle, via pipework running through to a manifold assembly behind the instrument panel and then on to the instruments themselves. Static pressure is piped to this manifold from two static vent holes positioned flush with the skin on either side of the rear fuselage beneath the engine decking area.

As the aircraft moves through the air, so its velocity causes an increase in pressure within the pitot system and this change is registered on the airspeed indicators. The static vents are sensitive to changes in pressure caused by changes in altitude. This affects readings on the barometric altimeters, vertical speed indicator and also the barometric airspeed indicators.

Observer's instrument panel

The Observer's instrument panel is positioned on the left-hand side of the cockpit. Not having any physical control of the aircraft, many of the instruments on the Pilot's panel are not duplicated, with the exception of a barometric

LEFT The pitot head installed just forward of the radome under the nose of the aircraft.

LEFT The static vent on the side of the rear fuselage, seen here with protective plug and tell-tale warning flag fitted.

LEFT The Observer's instrument panel.

1 Heading indicator
2 Airspeed indicator
3 Barometric altimeter
4 Floodlight dimmer
5 NVG map light
6 Radar display and control indicator
7 Flare dispense panel
8 M147 digital display control display unit
9 IR jammer control panel.

ABOVE The main
instrument panel.

1 Tactical Situation Display
2 Number 1 and 2 engine Nh tachometers
3 Number 1 and 2 engine T6 indicators
4 Number 1 and 2 engine oil pressure gauges
5 Number 1 and 2 engine oil temperature gauges
6 Fuel contents selector
7 Fuel contents gauge
8 Transmission oil pressure gauge
9 Transmission oil temperature gauge
10 MRGB oil shutter override switch
11 Master Armament Safety Switch (MASS)
12 Numbers 1, 2 and 3 hydraulic system pressure gauges
13 Nr and Nf triple tachometer
14 Weight on wheels switch
15 Guarded flare master arm switch.

altimeter, airspeed and heading indicators to aid with the navigation of the aircraft. It is therefore a relatively small panel. Immediately to the right of this, however, is the search radar CRT (cathode ray tube) screen and radar controls which dominate the area in front of the Observer. A short NVG-compatible stalk light is included which can be dimmed as required and allows the Observer to read maps and Flight Reference Cards (FRCs) at night.

Main instrument panel

Between the Observer's radar and the Pilot's panel is the main instrument panel. The left of this panel is dominated by the large Tactical Situation Display (TSD) screen. Beneath this

is the Number 2 remote frequency display. To the right is a parallel line of various temperature and pressure gauges grouped in pairs for the Number 1 (left) and Number 2 (right) engines: the two engine Nh tachometers, engine power turbine inlet temperature indicators, engine oil pressure gauges and the engine oil temperature gauges. Beneath these are the fuel selector switch and fuel contents gauge and below those are the hydraulic system pressure gauges for the three systems.

The combined tachometer sits to the right of the engine gauges and below that the transmission oil and pressure gauges. The Master Armament Safety Switch (MASS) is at the bottom right of the panel.

RIGHT Main
instrument panel
coaming

1 Compass correction card
2 Standby compass
3 Missile approach warning system switch
4 ESM controller indicator
5 Central warning panel (in the lit 'test' configuration)
6 Clock.

RIGHT The overhead console and engine control quadrant.

1 Miscellaneous switch panel
2 Engine anti-icing and lighting switches
3 Engine control panel
4 Fuel control panel
5 AC power control panel
6 DC power control panel
7 Rotor brake lever
8 Number 1 engine condition lever
9 Number 1 engine starter button and fire warning light
10 Speed select lever and Number 2 engine speed trimming knob
11 Number 2 engine condition lever
12 Number 2 engine starter button and fire warning light
13 Cabin air control lever
14 Cold start switch panel.

Running along the top of the main panel is the ESM indicator, the CWP, the radar-altimeter low-height audio warning indicator and finally the clock which can run for up to 24 hours and has a button-operated stopwatch function.

Those gauges relating to engine, gearbox and hydraulic systems have coloured areas around their circumferences to show the normal operating settings and limitations of each particular system: green denotes normal operating range, yellow indicates a precautionary zone and red is an operational limit.

On the centre windscreen pillar is mounted the fluid-filled, standby compass and its correction card. The compass also has its own built-in light source.

Overhead console

The overhead console contains switches to control external lighting, engine anti-icing, AC and DC electrical systems, fuel control and engine fire extinguishers.

LEFT Ground servicing switch panel marked 'for ground use only'.

RIGHT The interseat console.

1 Observer's CDNU
2 Pilot's CDNU
3 Miscellaneous switch panel
4 Ground speed and drift indicator
5 Observer's communication control panel
6 Observer's remote control unit
7 Auxiliary control panel
8 IFF/SSR control unit
9 Master erase switch panel
10 Compass controller
11 NVG cockpit lighting control and IR anti-collision switch
12 Cockpit lighting control panel
13 Pilot's communication control panel
14 Pilot's remote control unit
15 AFC engage controller
16 AFC test controller
17 Stores release panel
18 Cap over top of nose undercarriage oleo.

Interseat console

The interseat console between the Pilot and Observer houses the control boxes for the aircraft's radios, the two CDNUs, armament systems, automatic flying control system (AFCS) and cockpit lighting.

Cockpit lighting

All of the Lynx's cockpit instruments, with the exception of the standby compass and OAT gauge, have built-in lighting to allow them to be read in poor light or at night.

Ice accretion Vernier

Ice can pose a serious threat to the safety of any aircraft as it steadily and often imperceptibly builds up on the airframe or rotors. As it does so, the aerodynamic properties of the rotor blades can be altered and a loss of efficiency or even unbalancing can be caused, which could lead to structural failure. Any ice that becomes detached from the aircraft and is ingested by the engines can also cause a great deal of damage to the compressor and lead to engine failure.

To monitor this, an ice accretion Vernier is mounted on the outside of the cockpit on the right-hand side. This simple device consists of two slender metallic probes mounted one above the other and pointing into the airflow. The top probe is graduated into 11 divisions equating to up to 20cm thickness of ice build-up. The Pilot visually aligns a yellow datum line on the top probe with a corresponding yellow datum on the lower probe. The amount of ice that has built up on the bottom probe can then be measured visually against the scale on the top probe as the ice spreads along the bar.

Centralised Warning System

The Centralised Warning System (CWS) alerts the Pilot to any fault that might occur within systems that may affect the safety of the aircraft by collecting operating data from around the aircraft and sending electrical signals to the CWP. The CWP consists of a series of glass-fronted backlit captions in three colours designed to indicate their importance: green (advisory), amber (cautionary) and red (danger). Under normal operating conditions the panels remain unlit, but whenever a fault or a change occurs with any of the systems

LEFT The ice accretion Vernier fitted to the nose of the aircraft immediately below the Pilot's cockpit door.

being monitored, the corresponding caption will illuminate.

With an amber caption, an amber attention-getter button on the Pilot's instrument panel lights up; pressing this to acknowledge the fault clears the attention-getter but the caption remains on the CWP. Similarly, when a red caption illuminates on the CWP, a set of red attention-getter buttons marked 'CANCEL' illuminate on the instrument panel, but this time they are accompanied by an audio warning over the intercom. Pressing the button will cancel the attention-getters and the audio warning but the CWP light will still remain on. An anti-glare shield is fitted above the panel to shield the instruments from strong sunlight and thereby make any such warning captions easier to see.

Heating

The temperature of the cockpit air can be controlled via a cockpit-vent pull knob installed on the left side of the interseat console. Via a cable, this operates a valve in a control duct which is fed with fresh air from an external intake immediately in front of the windscreen or recirculated air from an internal intake above the

BELOW The Centralised Warning Panel in the lit 'test' configuration.

instrument panel. A blower motor pumps the air around ducting running behind the instrument panel, the tail rotor pedals and along both sides of the cockpit to a set of punkah louvres. A heater unit on the blower can be switched on to heat the air as it passes through.

For the cabin, an air scoop is fitted on the left-hand side of the fuselage beneath the Number 1 engine. A bleed of hot air from the engines is introduced into the air supply from the scoop via a mixer unit in the aft avionics bay and is pumped through ducting in the cabin roof to another set of punkah louvres above the cabin door. Shutter valves on the ducting within the cabin control the amount of air being fed into the cabin.

Lower fuselage

The main lower fuselage section is effectively a box made up from riveted and bolted aluminium alloy structure comprising longitudinal shear webs, transverse frames, cleats, fillets, diaphragms and stiffeners. It is divided into two sections. The forward bottom fuselage (which runs below and includes the cockpit floor) has removable panels to allow access to the flying control runs and nose undercarriage and provides areas for the installation of the radar altimeter antenna and forward flotation bag assemblies.

The main bottom fuselage includes the underside of the cabin floor through to forward of the undercarriage sponsons. Situated within the structure are three of the aircraft's five fuel tanks: the forward tank and the port and starboard collector tanks. Access to these tanks for maintenance is via circular panels on the cabin floor that are screwed into place. Removable panels on the underside also allow access to the tank sumps as well as their fuel and water drain valves.

Running fore and aft outboard of the lower fuselage box structure are angular D-shaped frames through which flying controls and electrical cabling run. These can be accessed via composite quick-release 'drop-down' panels hinged along their lower edges which, when

ABOVE The lower fuselage of the aircraft. Brackets can be used to mount either weapon carriers or troop steps on either side. A series of drop-down composite panels running along the lower edge allow easy access to the flying controls and electrical looms.

BELOW A series of drop-down, quick-release hinged panels run along the lower edge of the lower fuselage, giving access to wiring looms and some of the flying control components.

RIGHT The aluminium honeycomb cabin floor is protected from impact damage by a sheet of marine plywood with holes cut out to allow access to the freight tie-down rings. A small step is situated immediately aft of the interseat console (far right) to allow the Observer to climb from the cockpit when undertaking the role of Winchman. Beyond that is the *Orange Crop* ESM processor.

closed, also provide the external contouring of the lower fuselage.

On the underside of the lower fuselage is the attachment point for the Semi-Automatic Cargo Release Unit (SACRU).

The two sections are joined together with bolts and rivets immediately below the control frame.

Cabin

The aircraft's cabin area consists of the roof, the floor, the lower fuselage and the two sliding cabin doors.

Starting inside the cabin, the floor is made from an aluminium alloy honeycomb structure sandwiched between two sheets of aluminium alloy. Studs, recessed into the upper surface, allow the fitting of the cabin seating and various threaded inserts are positioned for the installation of ESM equipment and the overload tank if required. Strengthened tie-down points are also built into the floor to allow for the restraining of internal cargo.

Special quilted blankets are fitted to the internal sidewalls and internal roof to provide a degree of soundproofing, being held in place with Velcro strips. A large, hinged glass-reinforced plastic (GRP) fairing in the centre of the roof allows access to the underside of the main rotor gearbox (MRGB) and main rotor controls where they meet with the main rotor spindle lower attachment, as well as various electrical circuit-breaker boxes and relay panels.

The cabin doors are attached with pip pins at the top to brackets that run between two rows of steel ball-bearings in a track along the top of the cabin door aperture upper edge and by support brackets that run in the lower rail. A central horizontal rail is also included down the side of the fuselage aft of the door. These allow the doors to be slid rearwards to open. On the aft edge of the doors are shaped cam plates which engage with the retractable footsteps

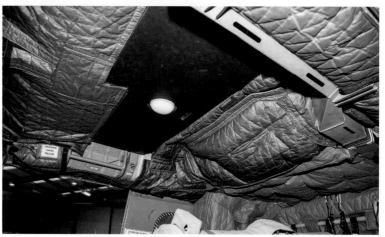

ABOVE The inside of the cabin roof showing the quilted soundproofing blankets. A cabin light is mounted in the centre panel.

BELOW The inside of the starboard cabin sliding door showing the jettisonable window assembly held in place by two spigots on the upper edge and identified as an emergency egress point by being marked with yellow and black diagonal lines. When the jettison lever immediately below the window is turned to the right in an emergency, lugs within the door holding the bottom edge of the window retract, enabling it to be pushed out to allow the cabin occupant to escape.

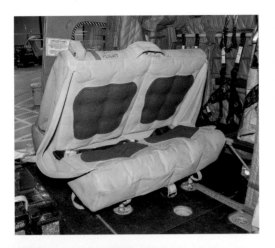

RIGHT Known affectionately as the 'bouncy castle' the four-man seat is made up from five inflatable cells. Although the ride is somewhat comfier than experienced in the front seats, when fully occupied it can be quite uncomfortable.

ABOVE Like the three-man seat, the six-man seat is of fabric and tube construction. Unlike the four-man seat (seen behind), however, it is fitted across the cabin with the occupants facing fore and aft.

on the outside of the fuselage and force them up into the closed position, thus preventing the door from being damaged. A spring-loaded flap and nylon roller on the lower edge of the door allows the door to open fully without hitting the undercarriage sponson. Each door has a large Perspex window, held in place by spigots, which can be jettisoned in an emergency by operating a handle either internally or externally. As with all emergency levers and buttons, these are marked with black and yellow diagonal stripes. They also have small, narrow luminous Beta lights to allow them to be located in the dark.

Seating

An inflatable troop seat, comprising of six individually inflated compartments, can be fitted to the cabin. In its normal fore-and-aft configuration it can seat up to four passengers – two either side – or one if positioned athwartships. Not renowned for its comfort, especially when all four positions are occupied, it is not surprisingly more commonly referred to as the 'bouncy castle'. However, this inflatable design does also provide a degree of additional buoyancy should the aircraft ditch into the sea.

Alternatively, a rigid six-man seat of fabric and tube construction can be installed. Unlike the four-man seat, it is fitted across the cabin with the occupants facing fore and aft. Like the four-man seat, simple airline-type lapstraps are provided.

Normally fixed along the rear of the cabin is a three-man seat, also of fabric and tube construction. Each position is fitted with a five-point harness.

Cabin roof

Now to the outside of the cabin areas. Joined to the control frame at the aft end of the cockpit, the roof is made from GRP. On the outer upper surface, control cables from the engine control quadrant in the cockpit run fore

LEFT The three-man seat, comprised of fabric stretched over aluminium alloy tubing, is fitted along the rear bulkhead in the cabin. Immediately underneath the MRGB, there is slightly less headroom – something to consider if you are tall! Each position has its own five-point harness.

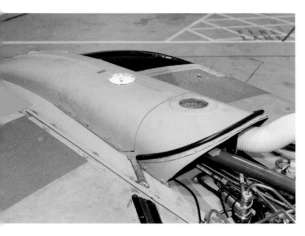

and aft along the centreline to the engines and the rotor brake. The controls themselves are protected by a series of hinged and detachable GRP fairings that form a tunnel. Areas either side of this tunnel that are suitably strengthened for maintainers to stand on are painted with grey anti-slip paint.

Giving protection to the MRGB, the hydraulic manifolds and control systems mounted on the cabin roof is the large sliding fairing. As the name suggests, this can be slid fore and aft on rails that are screwed to the roof to gain access to the transmission area. The fairing has small circular Perspex windows on either side to allow the fluid levels in both hydraulic reservoirs and the hydraulic accumulator pressures to be inspected without having to open the fairing. An

ABOVE LEFT The 'beak' fairing on top of the cockpit roof protects the engine controls. The white circular object is the GPS antenna.

ABOVE Spring-loaded hand-holds are built into the gutter assembly that runs along the upper edge of the cabin door aperture to assist with climbing in and out of the cabin.

BELOW LEFT When the external weapon carriers are not fitted, a step can be installed for trooping.

BOTTOM LEFT The sight glass for the Number 1 hydraulic system reservoir can be viewed from the port side through a window on the sliding fairing.

BELOW The hinged composite fairing protecting the Number 5 Tail Rotor Driveshaft (TRDS) can be seen here in the open position. The cover for the Intermediate Gearbox (IGB) has an open front end to scoop cooling air in and a grille at the top to allow it to escape.

LEFT Two foldaway footsteps are built into the side of the aircraft to allow access to the MRGB drop-down footstep panel and the engine servicing platform doors. Non-slip areas are also painted on to the upper surface of the sponsons to identify them as being suitable to stand on. A spring-loaded wedge on the lower rear section of the cabin door contains a roller which forces the wedge upwards when in contact with the sponson, thus allowing the door to open fully and not foul on the sponson.

intake and duct in the front channels air into the area to help cool the generators mounted to the accessory gearbox.

Rear fuselage

The rear fuselage, made from longerons, frames and stringers held together by an external aluminium alloy skin, extends from just ahead of the sponsons aft to the tailcone transportation joint. It is perhaps the most important part of the aircraft in that it carries the transmission and engine loads. It comprises the rear part of the cabin, the aft equipment bay and the engine compartments, and also provides sections that house the main fuel tanks, the harpoon and the attachments for the undercarriage sponsons.

To allow maintainers and aircrew to climb up the side of the aircraft for inspections, a series of foldaway steps are incorporated into the outer skins forward of the sponsons. These steps are held in the closed position during flight by spring-loaded bolts that are manually operated by pulling down on a ring. In the event that any of these steps are inadvertently left in the open position when either of the cabin doors are slid open, the cabin door trailing edge has a set of specially shaped cam plates which contact a strake on the footsteps and cause them to lift up into their closed positions to prevent the doors from becoming damaged.

Having climbed up the side, the maintainer or aircrew can then reach the latch to open the main rotor gearbox footstep fairing – so named because, when it is hinged open, it has a set of footsteps built into the inner face above the cabin door area. By standing on these, the main rotor head and gearbox area can be accessed and inspected.

RIGHT A shaped cam plate is fitted to the rear edge of both cabin sliding doors. Should the fold-down external footstep be left in the down position, the door could easily become damaged.

RIGHT To prevent this, a shaped cam on the rear edge of the door makes contact with a block on the footstep. The curvature of the cam causes the footstep to ride up …

RIGHT … and safely into the closed position.

ABOVE The starboard MRGB drop-down fairing in the open position showing the integral footstep arrangement (with grey anti-slip paint). The oil level sight glass for the MRGB itself can be seen.

ABOVE RIGHT The Number 1 (port) engine bay door in the open position. Braided metal lanyards hold the upper outer section of the door in position, while the lower section of the door rests against rubber blocks glued to the outside of the fuselage. The doors can be used as servicing platforms.

Aft equipment bay

The aft equipment compartment is accessed from underneath via a door aft of the undercarriage sponsons which hinges open outwards. Inside can be found racks containing radio equipment, the emergency flotation bottles, the aircraft battery, engine fire extinguisher bottles, electrical circuit-breaker panels and the tail rotor control cables.

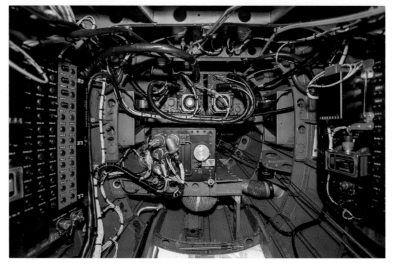

CENTRE The view inside the aft equipment bay looking forward. The flotation bottles and battery are in the lower foreground.

RIGHT The view inside the aft equipment bay looking aft.

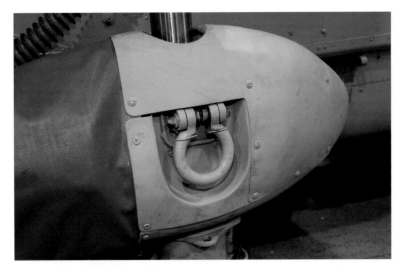

ABOVE Steel tie-down points allow the aircraft to be lashed down for security while the green cover protects the flotation bag contained within a small bay.

Sponsons

Running laterally through the rear fuselage are the aluminium alloy forward and rear spars and struts. Ribs attached to the ends of the spars allow aluminium skins to be riveted in place to produce an aerodynamic sponson. ESM aerial mounting positions are included on the trailing edge. The sponson structure provides the mounting points for the main undercarriage oleos and also for steel rings to allow the aircraft to be lashed down to a ship's flight deck, as well as recesses into which the rear flotation bags are housed.

BELOW Number 2 (starboard) engine door in the open position showing the air intake and exhaust scoop which feed the starter/generator and engine oil cooler ducts. The small grilles at the aft end allow ventilation of the engine bay. Because the starter/generator and oil cooler are fitted on the left-hand side of both engines, the scoops on port and starboard doors are not symmetrical.

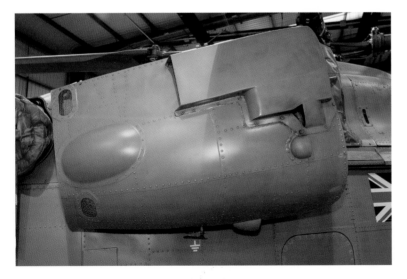

Engine area

Both of the engine bay doors are made up of two sections – an upper and a lower – joined together by a hinge. The lower section is itself attached to the engine bay decking via another hinge. When the door is opened, the lower section folds outwards on itself until it is parallel with the aircraft's skin, being held off the side of the rear fuselage by small rubber blocks. The upper section is then held suspended at right angles to the lower section by braided wire lanyards attached to the front and rear firewalls. Aluminium plating on the inside faces of the upper sections form walkways to allow maintainers to access the engine. The plating is painted in a rough anti-slip paint to provide a good grip for anyone standing on the doors. When closed, the doors are held in place with spigots operated by a retractable handle on the side and by a central 'T' handle on the upper edge of the central firewall.

The engine bays comprise a floor and three separate firewalls: a forward firewall, isolating the engines from the MRGB area; a rear firewall, separating the engine bay from the engine exhausts; and a central firewall, screening the two engines from each other. The front firewall is in two sections with the upper section forming the rear face of the air intake assembly. The centre firewall has a bulged lower section which forms a tunnel through which the tail rotor driveshaft passes.

The engine air intake is in two sections: an upper and a lower. The mouth of the intake assembly contains an electrically heated element to prevent ice from forming and being ingested into the engine. A metal mesh-type grille is also fitted in front of the intake to prevent the ingestion of anything that could otherwise cause foreign object damage (FOD).

Tail unit

The tail comprises three major components: the tailcone, the tail pylon and the tailplane.

Tailcone

The tailcone is a tapered cylindrical tube made up of two rolled aluminium alloy skins – an upper and lower – which overlap each other and are then riveted together through a series

of frames, half frames and plates, which give the tailcone its rigidity. It is attached at the forward end (known as the transportation joint) to the rear fuselage by 32 nuts and bolts.

Running along the top surface are the brackets to support the Numbers 3 and 4 tail rotor driveshafts on their way to driving the intermediate gearbox fitted at the base of the tail pylon. Hydraulic pipes for the tail rotor servo and electrical cables are clipped into and on to cleats along the upper surface, with everything being protected by curved reinforced plastic honeycomb covers that are hinged to allow access.

A series of three removable panels in the side of the tailcone allow internal maintenance access to the tail rotor control cables, cable tension regulator, pulleys and fairleads for adjustments and for inspection.

During the conversion to HMA Mk.8, additional strengthening external doubler plates and internal stringers were incorporated into the tailcone around the transportation joint and the tail pylon mounting lugs were reinforced to help to absorb the additional increase in power brought about by the change in rotational direction of the tail rotor.

Tail pylon

Like the tailcone, the tail pylon is made from a series of aluminium alloy frames and stringers held in place by an aluminium alloy outer skin. The forward end is almost cylindrical to match with the aft end of the tailcone. The upper surface, however, is flat to accommodate the intermediate gearbox. Aft of this the tail pylon

ABOVE The tailcone showing the HF aerial masts (antenna removed), transponder and V/UHF aerials below and DSP antenna fitted on the fixed fairing on top. Numbers 2, 3 and 4 tail rotor driveshafts can be seen running from left to right.

blends to a box-like vertical structure, the upper end of which acts as the mounting for the tail rotor gearbox, tail rotor servo and tailplane.

A series of reinforced plastic honeycomb aerodynamic fairings are fitted to the tail pylon to protect the transmission components and flying controls. On the upper and forward faces

BELOW The transportation joint showing the reinforcing doubler plates that were introduced during the conversion from HAS Mk.3 to HMA Mk.8 to provide additional strength following the change to a reverse-direction tail rotor. To the left is one of the *Orange Crop* ESM antennae with protective cover and 'remove before flight' tell-tale flag.

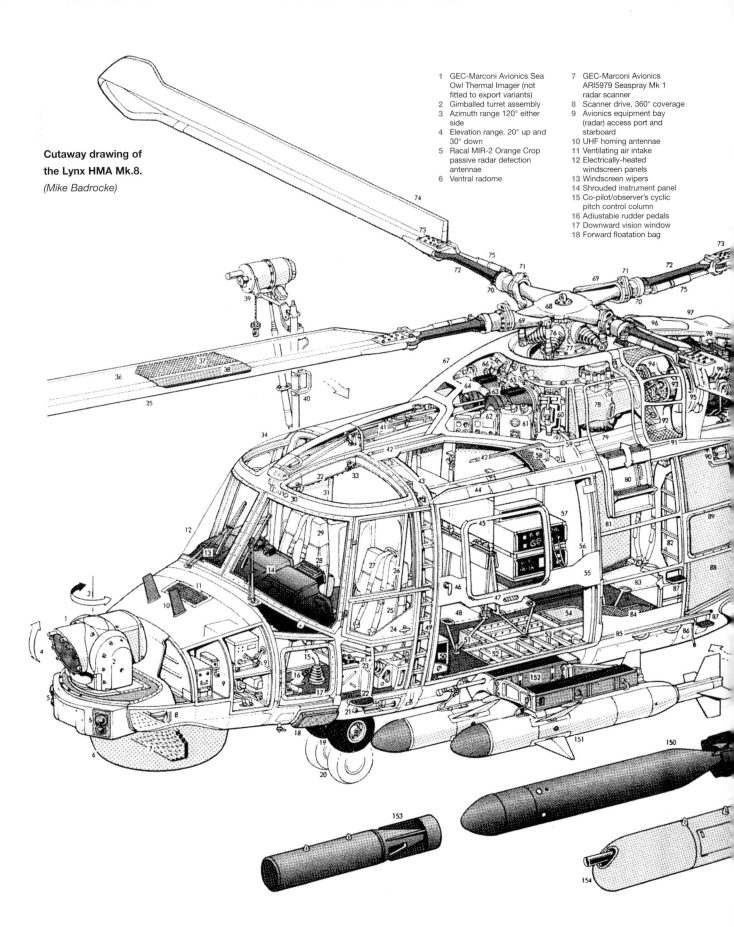

Cutaway drawing of the Lynx HMA Mk.8.

(Mike Badrocke)

1 GEC-Marconi Avionics Sea Owl Thermal Imager (not fitted to export variants)
2 Gimballed turret assembly
3 Azimuth range 120° either side
4 Elevation range. 20° up and 30° down
5 Racal MIR-2 Orange Crop passive radar detection antennae
6 Ventral radome
7 GEC-Marconi Avionics ARI5979 Seaspray Mk 1 radar scanner
8 Scanner drive, 360° coverage
9 Avionics equipment bay (radar) access port and starboard
10 UHF homing antennae
11 Ventilating air intake
12 Electrically-heated windscreen panels
13 Windscreen wipers
14 Shrouded instrument panel
15 Co-pilot/observer's cyclic pitch control column
16 Adiustabie rudder pedals
17 Downward vision window
18 Forward floatation bag

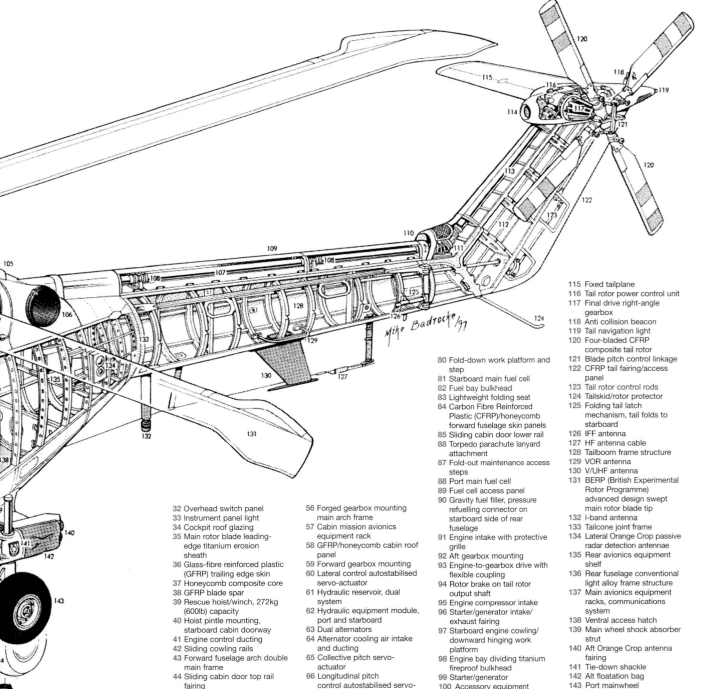

Mike Badrocke/97

80 Fold-down work platform and step
81 Starboard main fuel cell
82 Fuel bay bulkhead
83 Lightweight folding seat
84 Carbon Fibre Reinforced Plastic (CFRP)/honeycomb forward fuselage skin panels
85 Sliding cabin door lower rail
88 Torpedo parachute lanyard attachment
87 Fold-out maintenance access steps
88 Port main fuel cell
89 Fuel cell access panel
90 Gravity fuel filler, pressure refuelling connector on starboard side of rear fuselage
91 Engine intake with protective grille
92 Aft gearbox mounting
93 Engine-to-gearbox drive with flexible coupling
94 Rotor brake on tail rotor output shaft
95 Engine compressor intake
96 Starter/generator intake/exhaust fairing
97 Starboard engine cowling/downward hinging work platform
98 Engine bay dividing titanium fireproof bulkhead
99 Starter/generator
100 Accessory equipment gearbox
101 Forward main engine mounting
102 Titanium fireproof mounting deck
103 Rolls-Royce Gem 42-1 turboshaft engine
104 Starboard engine exhaust
105 Ventilating air exhaust duct
106 Port engine exhaust nozzle
107 Tail rotor transmission shaft
108 Shaft bearings
109 Hinged shaft access taiing
110 Cooling air intake
111 Intermediate gearbox
112 Tail pylon structure
113 Final dnve shaft
114 Gearbox cooling air intake

115 Fixed tailplane
116 Tail rotor power control unit
117 Final drive right-angle gearbox
118 Anti collision beacon
119 Tail navigation light
120 Four-bladed CFRP composite tail rotor
121 Blade pitch control linkage
122 CFRP tail fairing/access panel
123 Tail rotor control rods
124 Tailskid/rotor protector
125 Folding tail latch mechanism, tail folds to starboard
126 IFF antenna
127 HF antenna cable
128 Tailboom frame structure
129 VOR antenna
130 V/UHF antenna
131 BERP (British Experimental Rotor Programme) advanced design swept main rotor blade tip
132 I-band antenna
133 Tailcone joint frame
134 Lateral Orange Crop passive radar detection antennae
135 Rear avionics equipment shelf
136 Rear fuselage conventional light alloy frame structure
137 Main avionics equipment racks, communications system
138 Ventral access hatch
139 Main wheel shock absorber strut
140 Aft Orange Crop antenna fairing
141 Tie-down shackle
142 Alt floatation bag
143 Port mainwheel
144 Mainwheel rebound position and castoring angle
145 Torque scissor links
146 Port mainwheel sponson
147 Ventral Doppler antenna fairing
148 Ventral hydraulic deck-lock harpoon
149 Torpedo parachute housing
150 Sting Ray lightweight homing torpedo
151 Sea Skua anti-ship missiles
152 Weapons pylons, single or dual weapons fit
153 Mk 11 depth charge
154 FN HMP 12.7mm (1/2in) self-defence machine-gun pod

32 Overhead switch panel
33 Instrument panel light
34 Cockpit roof glazing
35 Main rotor blade leading-edge titanium erosion sheath
36 Glass-fibre reinforced plastic (GFRP) trailing edge skin
37 Honeycomb composite core
38 GFRP blade spar
39 Rescue hoist/winch, 272kg (600lb) capacity
40 Hoist pintle mounting, starboard cabin doorway
41 Engine control ducting
42 Sliding cowling rails
43 Forward fuselage arch double main frame
44 Sliding cabin door top rail fairing
45 Jettisonable window panel
46 Door latch
47 Window jettison handle
48 Lightweight demountable cabin seats
49 Right control rod linkages
50 ESM pulse receiver
51 Forward underfloor fuel cells, total usable capacity 957 litres (210 Imp gal) with gravity fuelling. 985 litres (217 Imp gal) with pressure refuelling
52 Cabin floor frame structure
53 Fuselage keel web
54 Fuel collector tanks (two)
55 Port rearward sliding cabin door

56 Forged gearbox mounting main arch frame
57 Cabin mission avionics equipment rack
58 GFRP/honeycomb cabin roof panel
59 Forward gearbox mounting
60 Lateral control autostabilised servo-actuator
61 Hydraulic reservoir, dual system
62 Hydraulic equipment module, port and starboard
63 Dual alternators
64 Alternator cooling air intake and ducting
65 Collective pitch servo-actuator
66 Longitudinal pitch control autostabilised servo-actuator
67 Forward-sliding equipment bay cowling
68 Hingeless main rotor hub, titanium
69 Blade pitch control horns
70 Pitch bearings
71 Individual bearing oil reservoirs
72 Flexible blade arm
73 Blade root attachment joint, manually foldable
74 Four-bladed main rotor
75 Drag hinge dampers
76 Blade pitch control rods
77 Main rotor mast
78 Main gearbox
79 Gearbox mounting deck

19 Fixed castoring twin-wheel nose undercarriage
20 Nosewheel rebound position
2f Port navigation light
22 Boarding step
23 Collective pitch lever
24 Jettisonable cockpit door, port and starboard
25 Co-pilot/observer's seat
26 Direct vision sliding side window panel
27 Safety harness
28 Shrouded radar display
29 Pilot's seat
30 Engine power and condition levers
31 Starboard sliding cabin door

RIGHT The tail fold ratchet assembly on the port side of the tailcone with the ratchet handle out of its spring-loaded retainer. The end of the ratchet assembly has a small lever which, when rotated through 180 degrees, changes the direction in which the ratchet operates, moving the locking pins either in or out.

are hinged semicircular covers for the Number 5 tail rotor driveshaft, while a wedge-shaped fairing known as the 'knife edge' is attached with screws to the trailing edge of the pylon to protect the flying control rods that run to the tail rotor servo. This fairing is also shaped to produce an aerodynamic effect, generating a lateral force to starboard as the aircraft's speed increases, thus reducing some of the effort required of the tail rotor to maintain directional control. A spring-loaded panel built into this fairing allows easy access to the spring bias unit. Separate fairings with grilles and intakes to aid cooling and apertures through which the oil sight level glasses can be seen are also

attached over the intermediate gearbox, tail rotor gearbox and servo unit to complete the assembly – the latter being known, because of its shape, as the 'bullet fairing'.

The tail pylon is designed with four male attachment lugs and bushes on the forward frame that mate with corresponding female fork-end fittings on the aft frame of the tailcone. The starboard attachments are bolted to form a hinge, while those on the port side are held securely in place by a special retractable bolt arrangement. This mechanism is operated by a ratchet assembly, permanently fitted to the aft port side of the tailcone, which moves a set of stainless steel pins that engage vertically through the fork-ends to link with the lugs to secure the tail pylon in place.

By reversing the direction of the ratchet, the pins can be retracted to allow the port lugs to disengage in order for the pylon to fold to starboard through 170 degrees where it is held in place by a latch-back mechanism fitted to the starboard side of the tailcone. This effectively reduces the overall length of the aircraft for easy stowage in ships' hangars. It also has the added benefit of reducing the

RIGHT With the Number 4 drive shaft cover open, the 'PIN OUT' warning flag can be seen in its stowed position, pivoted into place by a striker coming into contact with the locking pin when in the locked position.

FAR RIGHT With the locking pin retracted and the tail pylon folded, the 'PIN OUT' flag has sprung back to show that the pins are unlocked.

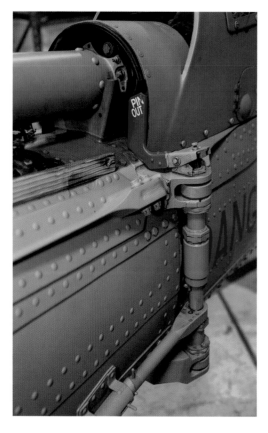

FAR LEFT The latch-back spigot on the starboard side of the tail pylon …

LEFT … and spring-loaded mechanism on the tailcone for securing the tail pylon in the folded position.

space that the aircraft takes up in the hangar while ashore.

Tailplane

Attached to the upper end of the tail pylon is a horizontal tailplane, otherwise known as a stabiliser. Made from composite materials that are moulded and bonded together and fitted around a spar held in place by a set of clamps, it helps to provide longitudinal stability in forward flight.

With the change to CMRBs, it was found that their BERP tips generated aerodynamic vortices which interfered with the effectiveness of the tailplane. To rectify this, the tailplane

was shortened in span and a device known as a Gurney flap incorporated into the trailing edge. This simple right-angled piece of metal improves the performance of the tailplane by increasing the pressure on the pressure face and decreasing pressure on the suction face, thus generating more downforce.

BELOW The horizontal stabiliser with spar mounted through a set of clamps on the top of the tail pylon. The right-angled Gurney flap arrangement can be seen on the trailing edge of the stabiliser. The tail rotor hydraulic actuator is mounted above the spar.

1	Tail rotor gearbox	3	Horizontal stabiliser spar and clamp	4	Yaw control rod
2	Tail rotor servo			5	'Knife edge' fairing

6 Horizontal stabiliser
7 Gurney flap.

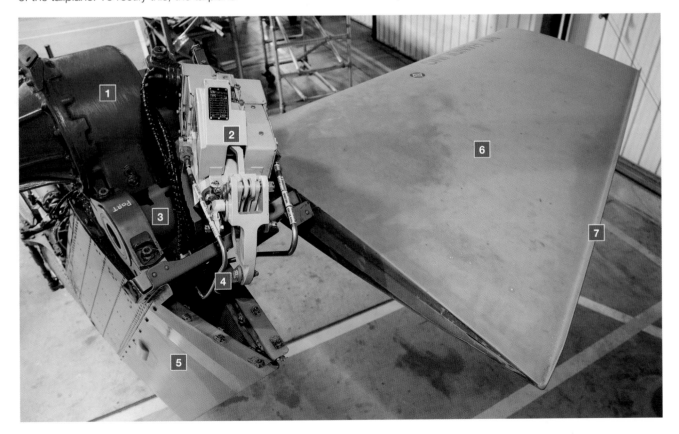

ABOVE The bolted main rotor head showing the central lifting eye.

BELOW The yellow blade arm can be seen fitting into the blade sleeve. The lag plane damper connects between the blade sleeve and 'dog bone' extension arm, via a trunnion, to the main rotor blade.

Main rotor system

Main rotor head

The Lynx is designed with a semi-rigid main rotor head comprising a hub, a mast, a pitch control spider, four blade sleeves with extension arms, four dampers and four pitch control rods, the operation of which will be covered later. Unlike conventional articulated heads which have drag and flapping hinges that absorb flight loads, with a semi-rigid main rotor these are replaced with titanium elements that have the ability to flex. This gives a substantial improvement in maintenance requirements and flying characteristics.

The 'bolted' main rotor head, which replaced the original one-piece 'monobloc' head, comprises two forged titanium pieces: a central hub disc and a mast. The hub, which has a lug bolted to its upper surface that can be used to lift not only the head by itself but the head and MRGB together or even the whole aircraft, effectively controls flap (movement up and down). It is attached with 16 bolts to the hub mast which has narrow vertical slots through which the four arms of the pitch control spider protrude.

Blade sleeves, filled with oil and topped up from their own small reservoir attached externally via a band, are fixed to the arms of the hub disc. These are held in place with parallel roller bearings and by tie bars, which are themselves made from continuous lengths of stainless steel wire wrapped around bobbins. These tie bars are immensely strong, having to withstand the huge centrifugal forces trying to pull the main rotor blades from the head. Indeed, failure of any one of these bars would result in the loss of a blade and the loss of the aircraft, including the crew. Routine inspections for corrosion and checking for any instance of overspeeding of the main rotor, which would over-stress the bars and reduce their strength, are therefore a vital part of the maintenance regime for the aircraft.

Bolted to the outer end of the tie bars are the blade extension arms. These solid titanium arms – sometimes referred to as the 'dog bone' due to the shape of the outer end on to which

the main rotor blades attach – control the main rotor blade drag (movement fore and aft).

Between each of the blade sleeves and the 'dog bone' end of the extension arms are hydraulic blade dampers. Attached to the end of the arm by a trunnion assembly, these control the rate of movement of the blade extension arms in drag by forcing hydraulic fluid through a restrictor valve as the blade extension arm starts to drag backwards.

Pitch control spider

Converting the linear movements generated by the Main Rotor Actuators (MRAs) to control inputs acting on the rotating main rotor head is the job of the pitch control spider assembly. Fitted inside the hollow main rotor head mast, a spindle within a splined sleeve is made to move via inputs from the MRAs. A gimbal ring near the top of the spindle impinges on the inner ends of the spider arms protruding through the rotating mast assembly. This ring allows the vertical movement of the non-rotating spindle to act on the ends of the rotating spider arms, causing them to move up or down. The spider arms themselves are protected by rubber boots attached to a shroud around the mast body.

Pitch control rods

Pitch control rods (PCRs) connect the outer ends of the arms to a horn on the end of the blade sleeves. This vertical movement of the rods causes the sleeves to rotate and thus alters the pitch of the main rotor blades. The PCRs are adjustable to allow rigging of the main rotor to be carried out.

Cyclic inputs cause the spindle to tilt, altering the pitch on individual blades only and generating pitch and roll manoeuvres. When a cyclic input is generated, however, the whole spindle slides up or down the splined ring inside, and impinges on all four of the spider arms, causing pitch changes on all four blades and allowing the aircraft to climb or descend.

The whole hub and mast assembly is

RIGHT The spider control arms protruding through the mast collar and protected by rubber boots. Seen here is the red pitch-change rod attached to the red blade sleeve.

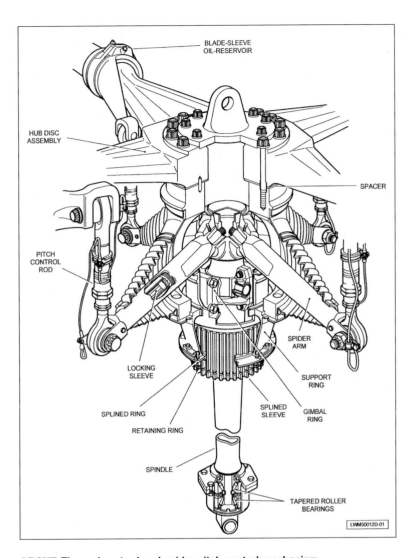

ABOVE **The main rotor head spider pitch control mechanism.** *(AP101C-1308-1D1)*

BRITISH EXPERIMENTAL ROTOR PROGRAMME (BERP) BLADES AND G-LYNX

Developed in a joint venture between Westland and the Ministry of Defence at the Royal Aerospace Establishment (RAE) Farnborough, an initial feasibility study conducted as long ago as 1974 into the use of composite main rotor blades had led to the production of a construction technique demonstrator four years later. Known as the British Experimental Rotor Programme (BERP), a Lynx CMRB was first fabricated in 1981. With a 'paddle' tip design that raised the speed at which the effect of sonic vibration at the tip of the advancing blade occurred (at the same time as delaying the onset of reverse airflow at the top of the retreating blade), the composite structure also gave better in-service life, enhanced stress dispersion characteristics and a greater resilience to withstanding battle damage.

Flight trials began in August 1985 with the first production Lynx AH Mk.7, XZ170, and showed that the speed benefits gained with the new blades, coupled with a sufficiently improved engine performance, had the potential to allow Westland to mount a successful bid to recapture the helicopter airspeed world record from the Soviet Union. The prestige

associated with this accolade, it was hoped, would boost foreign sales of the Lynx.

Chosen to undertake the attempt, the company demonstrator aircraft – ZB500 – had originally been built in 1979 to the same standard as the AH Mk.1, but by virtue of being subjected to the many and varied trials programmes in the intervening years had become something of a hybrid.

Work to prepare the aircraft for the attempt on the record included the replacement of the existing main rotor gearbox with a Westland WG-30 unit re-rated to accept 2,498shp. Driving this was a pair of experimental 1,200shp Gem 60 engines fitted with water/methanol injection to increase their power output. All protruding objects on the fuselage were faired over to reduce aerodynamic drag and a new low-set tailplane with endplate fins – also robbed from a WG-30 – was fitted to offload the tail rotor at high airspeeds.

On 11 August 1986 – just one year and two days after the first flight of the BERP blades, and now suitably re-registered as G-LYNX, Westland's latest Chief Test Pilot, Trevor Egginton and his Flight Test Engineer, Derek Clews, broke the absolute speed record with a recorded average after two runs of a special course across the Somerset Levels of 249.09mph – a record that still stands to this day.

The first production BERP CMRBs began to emerge in 1989 and were initially fitted to the new Lynx AH Mk.9 variant. Subsequently they were embodied on all marks of Lynx to become the standard type of blade.

G-LYNX was eventually retired in 1992 and donated to the Helicopter Museum at Weston-super-Mare, being restored to her original record-breaking configuration by apprentices at AgustaWestland in 2012.

BELOW The FAI certificate for the helicopter airspeed world record achieved by G-LYNX on 11 August 1986. *(via AgustaWestland)*

attached directly to the output of the main rotor gearbox by 16 bolts held within recesses that are safety wirelocked together in pairs: a notoriously fiddly and frustrating job that many Lynx maintainers have grown to hate! A flexible enamel dark grey paint is applied to the head to afford some environmental protection to the titanium surface.

Main rotor blades

The Lynx main rotor turns anti-clockwise when viewed from above. The four main rotor blades are of composite construction, made from glass and carbon fibre materials impregnated with a thermosetting resin. Each blade comprises a glass and carbon fibre box-section spar wrapped around a foam core, which is then sealed by a woven glass scrim for protection. This spar tapers, becoming thicker at the root end to give the blade stiffness and added mass. When the spar has been assembled, heat and pressure are applied to cure the materials and produce a 'D' shape to the assembly. Titanium sideplates are attached to the root end to form the blade cuff and are secured in place by 11 nuts and bolts. These cuffs have large holes for the main rotor blade attachment pins to assemble the blades to the main rotor head.

Bonded to the spar, a sandwich of honeycomb core, carbon fibre and woven glass fibre forms the aerodynamic trailing edge of the blade. A special aluminium 'Astro Strike' material is also included along the outer section of each blade to conduct electricity away harmlessly in the event of the aircraft being struck by lightning.

As the blades rotate at high speed, any rain, salt or sand in the air can become highly erosive to the leading edge of the blades and rapidly shorten their lives. Two titanium leading edge strips are therefore bonded to the leading edge of the spar running along 80% of the length of each blade for protection against such environmental erosion. A small braided metal lead ensures electrical bonding between the sideplates and the erosion shields. On the enlarged, anhedral BERP tip, the quadrant and extreme tip shields made from electro-formed nickel are fitted for the same purpose.

Any rotating component, of course, needs to be finely balanced to prevent vibration – which

in some cases can ultimately lead to structural failure. To achieve this balance the main rotor blades have weights that are installed in the BERP tip and along a bar inside a tube running the full length of the spar inside the leading edge.

Transmission

The purpose of the Lynx's transmission system is to translate the power from the engines into mechanical movement to drive the main and tail rotors, thereby generating lift and thrust. The transmission system comprises four main elements: the main rotor gearbox; a tail rotor driveshaft in five sections; an intermediate gearbox; and a reduction tail rotor gearbox.

ABOVE The BERP tip of the CMRB showing the titanium erosion strip.

BELOW The main rotor gearbox with cowlings removed and access panels opened. The gold-coloured housing contains the oil filter.

ABOVE A view from the port side of the MRGB showing the Number 1 engine input coupling and gimbal ring assembly. The main rotor head cowling can be seen (left) with drain tube installed. With the air intake assemblies removed, the engine intake has had red blanks inserted to prevent any contamination by foreign objects.

Main rotor gearbox

The main rotor gearbox, mounted on two steel horizontal I-beam castings on the cabin roof and secured in place by four bolts, is made from magnesium alloy. Power from both engines, which are themselves attached to the forward face of the gearbox via gimbal rings and couplings, drives a system of bevel, load sharing and conformal pinions, reducing the input speed from the engines to turn the main rotor hub and tail rotor take-off drive.

Providing positive drive to the conformal pinions under normal operation, two input freewheels automatically disconnect the drive in the event of an engine failure – a condition known as freewheeling – to isolate the faulty engine from the gearbox. The port freewheel unit has a secondary purpose during engine start which is described in the section entitled 'Accessory drive'.

A two-part GRP dished fairing is bolted to the top of the gearbox when installed.

CONFORMAL GEARS

Conformal gears use 'area contact' of meshing in comparison with traditional involute gearing, which uses 'point contact'. In doing so, greater loads can be transmitted at each reduction stage, meaning fewer stages are required to achieve the same result. This, in turn, means that the gearbox can be lighter. Fewer gears also mean a smaller gearbox with reduced gear friction.

This fairing mates with the sliding fairing and engine air intake assemblies to act as a sort of gutter, collecting water and allowing it to flow overboard through a small drain tube to protect the gearbox area from water ingress.

Oil system

The MRGB is lubricated by between 26 and 29 litres (depending on modification status) of OEP215 oil pumped from the sump around the gearing and casing by a mechanically driven oil pump mounted on the accessories gearbox. A long, thin sight glass on the left-hand side of the gearbox casing allows the level of oil to be checked.

A 50-micron filter contained within a housing attached to the right-hand side of the casing is designed to try to prevent any foreign matter from contaminating the system (which might cause a blockage and therefore interfere with the lubrication). A mechanical indicator is fitted to the top of the filter which the maintainer will check to see if it has popped up, indicating if any blockage has occurred.

After flowing through the filter, the oil passes to a Marston Palmer cooler matrix mounted on an angled duct casting at the rear of the MRGB. The duct contains a fan that is mechanically driven from the tail take-off pinion gear and which draws air through the matrix to cool the oil. An electrically operated 90-degree rotary actuator governed by a sensor in the oil cooler head operates a set of three vanes within the duct to control the cooling of the oil. When the sensor detects the oil rising to 66°C, the actuator will open the vanes to allow more air to be drawn through and increase the cooling. If the temperature drops to 47°C the vanes will be closed to allow the oil to heat up again. A bypass valve in the system ensures that on start-up the cold – and therefore more viscous – oil is not fed through the cooler. Having been drawn through the matrix to cool the oil, this air is then fed into the MRGB area to help to cool the MRGB outer casing.

Giving all-important indications on the oil system is the oil temperature gauge on the left-hand side of the Pilot's instrument panel which has a scale between –50°C and +160°C; above this is the oil pressure gauge which reads in bar.

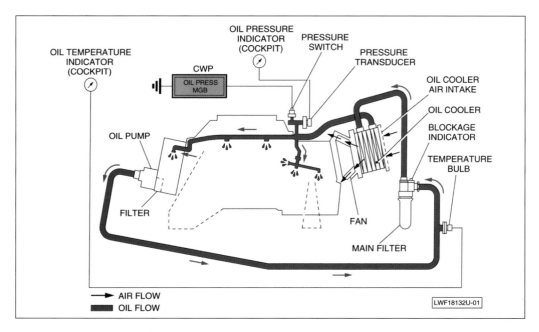

LEFT Main rotor
gearbox oil
system schematic.
(AP101C-1308-15C)

When the oil pressure, sensed by a pressure transmitter, drops below 1.38bars (20psi) a red 'OIL PRESS MGB' caption will illuminate on the Pilot's CWP. This will extinguish when the pressure rises above 1.72bar (25psi).

Accessory drive

As well as driving the main and tail rotors, the MRGB also has to provide drive to the Number 1 and Number 2 alternators for AC electrical power generation, Number 1 and Number 2 hydraulic pumps and the spur gear

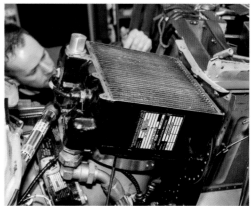

LEFT The Marston
Palmer oil cooler
matrix mounted on top
of the duct containing
a fan at the aft end of
the MRGB.

LEFT The accessory
drive actuator and its
associated armature
mounted on the rear
of the MRGB ahead of
the Number 1 engine
input coupling.

1 MRGB casing
2 Accessory drive actuator
3 Accessory drive actuator linkage
4 Number 1 engine input shaft
5 Number 1 engine gimbal
6 Number 1 engine air intake.

pressure and suction pumps serving the gearbox's own independent 26-litre (5.72-Imp gallon) oil system wet sump, pressure jets and an oil cooler.

Performing this function is the accessory drive gearbox that forms part of the front of the MRGB. The Number 1 and Number 2 engine input drives turn two through-shafts (port and starboard) and associated freewheel units which drive the gearbox and the equipment fitted to it. The starboard through-shaft has one tooth more on the meshing gears, which means that it runs at 69rpm faster than its port counterpart to provide a positive drive from the starboard side at all times.

The port freewheel unit is, however, different. When the Number 1 engine is started it is done so in what is called accessory drive – 'ACC DRIVE'. This is where the drive from the engine is allowed to turn gears within the MRGB to provide power to accessory systems while not driving the main rotor system itself. When starting the aircraft it is essential to have AC electrical and hydraulic power available, both of which are provided by operation of the accessories gearbox. Unlike the starboard freewheel unit, the port freewheel is actuated. Consisting of a set of rollers – contained within a circular housing controlled by an electro-mechanical actuator which can slide the rollers in and out of a corresponding set of roller cams – the freewheel allows the Number 1 engine to engage and disengage with the main drive and thereby provides essential services without the need to have the main rotor turning.

When the Pilot selects the 'ACC DRIVE/ MAIN DRIVE' switch on the cockpit overhead console to 'MAIN DRIVE', an electric motor in the accessory drive actuator, fitted to the rear left-hand side of the MRGB, operates a linkage assembly which moves a yoke attached to the roller housing. The housing then slides the rollers up against the cams until the two engage, causing the port through-shaft to begin to turn, providing power to the three-pinion assembly and turning the main rotor drive.

When the cockpit switch is deselected to 'ACC DRIVE', the linkage moves in the opposite direction to slide the roller housing back away from the cams, thus disconnecting the drive and stopping the main drive train, but still allowing the accessories gearbox to run to operate the various ancillary equipment even with the Number 2 engine and main rotor stopped.

Operating the accessory drive actuator can do a lot of damage to the MRGB if the correct sequence is not followed. If both engines are running at maximum power, the transfer from 'ACC DRIVE' to 'MAIN DRIVE' can cause what is known as a 'crash engagement' where too much energy is imparted into the gears at once. A series of electrical microswitches are included to minimise the chances of this happening, but following the correct procedure is still vital.

Rotor brake

A rotor brake assembly, consisting of a set of pads – one moving, one fixed – operated by a hydraulic piston and acting upon a steel disc, is attached to the Number 1 tail rotor driveshaft aft of the MRGB. The piston operating the moving brake pad is powered by the Number 3 hydraulic system and selected on and off by a lever on the left-hand side of the overhead console in the cockpit and a visual confirmation of its status is given via an amber caption on the CWP.

Tail rotor driveshafts 1–5

The Lynx has five driveshafts and an adaptor shaft made from heat-treated light-alloy tubes with bonded and riveted light-alloy end flanges with three holes for mounting bolts. Their purpose is to transmit the drive from the main rotor gearbox – via an intermediate gearbox and the tail rotor gearbox – to turn the tail rotor and thereby counteract the torque reaction generated by the main rotor to give directional control.

Beginning at the main rotor gearbox tail take-off output flange with the short stainless steel adaptor shaft, which is bolted to the aft face of the rotor brake disc assembly, Number 1 shaft passes between the two engines in a tunnel formed by the bulging-out of the bottom of the firewall. This has the added benefit of affording protection to the shaft in the event of an engine fire.

Emerging from the rear firewall into the area between the two engine exhausts, the alloy flanged aft end meets with the Number 2 shaft forward splined steel driving flange. Near the forward end of the shaft is an oil-filled titanium fitting containing needle roller bearings. The fitting features three mounting holes to allow it to be bolted to the support bracket.

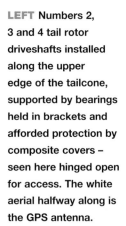

LEFT Numbers 2, 3 and 4 tail rotor driveshafts installed along the upper edge of the tailcone, supported by bearings held in brackets and afforded protection by composite covers – seen here hinged open for access. The white aerial halfway along is the GPS antenna.

Each of the shafts is attached to one another via flexible couplings: packs of between 10 and 14 thin spring steel shims designed to absorb any horizontal movement in the shafts. The packs have six holes around their circumference with the shafts being mounted to the coupling packs through alternate holes with three bolts on either end.

Number 2 shaft continues aft to join with Number 3 shaft, also with its own splined driving flange and intermediate bearing bolted to a support bearing at the forward end. A final support bracket, halfway along the top of the tailcone, allows Numbers 3 and 4 shafts to connect in a similar fashion.

Although Numbers 2, 3 and 4 shafts are nominally interchangeable, Number 4 differs slightly in having the female part of the special disconnect coupling bolted to the aft end through a flexible coupling pack.

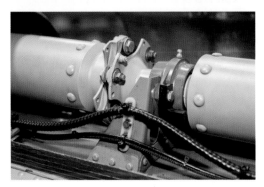

The final shaft in the transmission system is Number 5 driveshaft. Unlike the other shafts, this has fixed flanges at both ends and is mounted along the forward edge of the tail pylon between the intermediate gearbox output and tail rotor gearbox input flanges. Flexible coupling packs are also used to take up any adjustments in length between the two, being fitted at either end.

LEFT The Number 3 (left) driveshaft with flanged end attached through the flexible couplings to the flanged end of the Number 4 driveshaft. The latter is free to slide fore and aft on splines through the bearing (in dark grey) to allow for adjustments in end-float.

LEFT The Number 5 driveshaft running along the forward face of the tail pylon from the intermediate gearbox (right) to the tail rotor gearbox (upper left). Here the various cowlings and covers are open for maintenance.

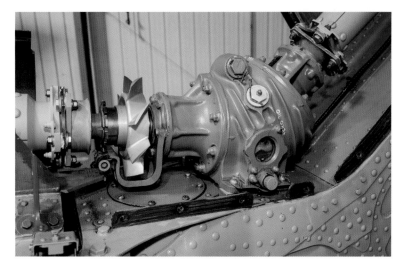

ABOVE The intermediate gearbox with its cowling removed showing the cooling fan and oil sight glass.

Intermediate gearbox and disconnect coupling

Fitted at the forward lower end of the tail pylon by four bolts, the intermediate gearbox (IGB) comprises three magnesium alloy sub-assemblies: an input, a centre and an output housing. Its purpose is to connect the Number 4 and Number 5 driveshafts and to change the direction of the tail rotor drive output from the main gearbox to the tail rotor gearbox.

At the forward end of the input shaft is the disconnect coupling assembly which, as the name suggests, allows the drive to the tail rotor to be easily disconnected for the purpose of

folding the tail pylon and reconnected when the pylon is spread. The coupling consists of a spring-loaded male connector (that mates with the end fitting on the Number 4 driveshaft when the tail pylon is spread) and a toothed locking plate fitted immediately aft of this which, when the tail is folded, is held in position by a spring-loaded locking lever that engages automatically to prevent the tail rotor from 'windmilling' in the wind.

A small fan is installed on the input shaft to provide cooling air to the outer surface of the gearbox, which is designed with cooling fins to aid the dissipation of heat. Running on taper bearings, the input shaft drives an input pinion gear which meshes with an outer pinion gear fitted to the output shaft.

The gearbox has a 0.65-litre (0.142-Imp gallon) oil capacity OX26 wet sump system into which the pinion gears are partially immersed. As the gears rotate, so they splash oil around to provide lubrication to themselves and the roller bearings. Oil is replenished via a nipple on the centre housing and the level can be checked via a sight glass on the left-hand side. This glass has two lines on it: green for full and red for low level. The lines have a kink halfway along to take into account the change in angle of the tail pylon when it is spread and folded

RIGHT The female disconnect coupling at the end of the Number 4 driveshaft has a striker plate which engages with the gust lock mechanism on the male coupling, holding the Number 5 driveshaft stationary when the pylon is folded and moving the lock out of position when the pylon is spread again.

RIGHT The male part of the disconnect coupling attached to the input shaft for the TRGB showing the locking mechanism and the cooling fan used to help cool the gearbox.

MAGNETIC CHIP DETECTORS

Predicting and detecting any component breakdown in the main, intermediate or tail rotor gearboxes is obviously vitally important in order to avoid any catastrophic failure which may lead to the loss of the aircraft and, potentially, the crew. Immersed into the gearbox's oil sump, the plug's magnetic inner core attracts any ferrous particles that may be present within the oil and, as it courses through the gearbox, these clump together on the plug. These plugs are checked for signs of ferrous debris by the groundcrew. If any is found, samples are taken and sent away for analysis to determine which component they have come from.

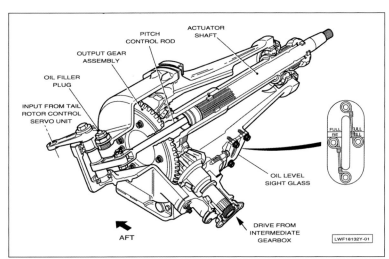

so that accurate readings can be taken in any configuration. A self-sealing drain plug with built-in magnetic chip detector is fitted on the left-hand side of the centre housing.

Tail rotor gearbox

The magnesium alloy tail rotor gearbox (TRGB) is mounted to a flat platform at the upper end of the tail pylon by eight bolts. Its main functions are:

- To take the input from the Number 5 driveshaft and reduce the rotational input speed.
- To change the angle of drive through 90 degrees to drive the tail rotor hub.

- To provide a mounting for the tail rotor itself.
- To hold the tail rotor pitch change mechanism itself.

Similar to the IGB, the TRGB is made up from separate housings: an input and an output. As with the IGB, pinion gearing is also splash lubricated using its own independent 0.90-litre (0.197-Imp gallon) capacity wet sump which is topped up through a filler plug. A self-sealing drain plug with magnetic chip detector is also fitted, together with a sight glass. Unlike the IGB, however, this can only be accurately checked when the pylon is spread.

ABOVE LEFT The tail rotor gearbox with cowling installed, showing the cooling duct in the leading edge and the slot through which the gearbox oil level sight glass can be inspected.

ABOVE Cutaway drawing of the tail rotor gearbox. *(ETS Yeovilton)*

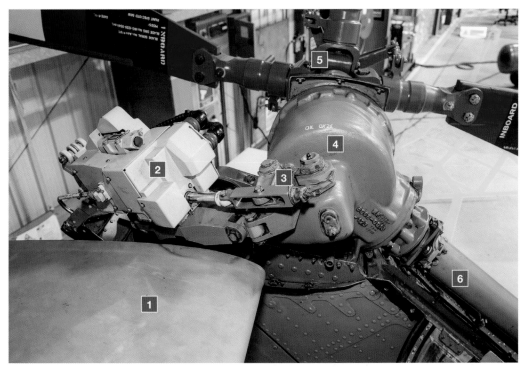

LEFT The tail rotor actuator with operating linkage attached to the input housing of the tail rotor gearbox.

1 Horizontal stabiliser
2 Tail rotor servo
3 Tail rotor gearbox pitch control arm
4 Tail rotor gearbox
5 Tail rotor hub
6 Number 5 tail rotor driveshaft.

ABOVE The tail rotor pitch change beam, held in place on the end of the tail rotor gearbox output shaft by a nut, is made to move in and out by the hydraulic actuator. This action pulls and pushes the short pitch change rods which cause the arms to rotate, thus altering the pitch of the tail rotor blades to increase or decrease anti-torque thrust.

BELOW The four-bladed, clockwise-rotating tail rotor assembly.

The input shaft has a flanged end that attaches, via flexible couplings, to the output flange of the Number 5 driveshaft. The output shaft, however, has splines to allow the fitting of the tail rotor hub. As well as providing drive to the tail rotor hub, the horizontal output shaft is designed to allow a solid, adjustable, splined pitch-control shaft to move axially through its hollow centre to operate the pitch change beam. A more detailed description of its operation can be found in the section entitled 'How a helicopter flies'.

Tail rotor hub

The tail rotor hub assembly is made up of a central titanium hub forging, about which are mounted four flapping hinge assemblies. The hub is internally splined to allow it to be mounted on to the tail rotor gearbox output shaft. Each of the four flapping hinges are made from a flapping link, which allows the tail rotor blade to flap, and a blade sleeve which incorporates the feathering hinge and a tie bar that absorbs the axial loads. The blade sleeves have forked ends that allow the tail rotor blades to be attached. Long, threaded 'preponderance bars' protrude outwards from each of the blade sleeves; these were designed to have external weights fitted to them to assist with the balance of the tail rotor, but are no longer used.

Pitch change beam

Attached to the end of the tail rotor gearbox output shaft is the pitch change beam that includes four pitch change rods. These rods connect to the blade sleeves. When the output shaft moves, so the pitch change beam causes the rods to push/pull on the blade sleeves and make them rotate, achieving a change of pitch on the tail rotor blades.

Tail rotor blades

The four tail rotor blades are of similar construction to the main rotor blades, using glass and carbon fibre materials for strength, bonded around a D-section spar. The four blades are attached to the forked ends of the tail rotor hub blade sleeves by two bolts and are identified by coloured strips to ensure that they are positioned correctly. Unlike previous variants, the Lynx HMA Mk.8 tail rotor turns

FAR LEFT One of the four tail rotor blades with red and white markings to increase its visibility when rotating. A titanium strip runs along the leading edge to give protection from erosion.

LEFT The spring bias unit (with upper link disconnected) on the aft face of the tail pylon helps to offset some of the aerodynamic forces acting on the tail rotor.

clockwise when viewed from the left-hand side.

Spring bias unit

A powerful spring attached to a piston and contained within a cylinder, mounted on the aft face of the tail pylon and connected into the yaw control system, helps the Pilot to overcome some of the high aerodynamic forces generated when trying to operate the tail rotor pedals. It also gives automatic control over yaw application in the event of a hydraulic failure. Under normal conditions, the Number 1 hydraulic system is capable of overcoming the spring pressure and the system is kept in balance. If the pressure drops, however, the spring overcomes the hydraulic system acting upon it, allowing the piston to extend and increasing tail rotor thrust.

It is important to ensure that this spring is not under compression after the aircraft has shut down, in order to prevent it from activating while a maintainer has their fingers in the way.

Flying controls

How a helicopter flies

For any type of aircraft to fly, it first needs to overcome the force of gravity acting upon its own weight. To do this it has to generate an equal opposing force known as lift.

In a conventional aeroplane, lift is generated by virtue of the aerodynamic properties of the aerofoil shape of the wings altering the pressure of the air flowing above and below it as the aircraft is propelled forward.

A helicopter, of course, has no such conventional wings. Instead, this lift is produced by the aerofoil-shaped main rotor blades being spun at high speed through the air. This means that, unlike a fixed-wing aircraft, the helicopter is not reliant on forward motion in order to create lift and can therefore take off and land vertically, as well as hover and even fly backwards.

But for a helicopter to achieve controlled flight, three basic primary flying controls are required: cyclic, collective and yaw.

Cyclic control

As the rotor blades rotate they prescribe a horizontal disc with lift being generated at 90 degrees to it. By altering the angle of this disc, the movement and direction of the helicopter can be controlled: forward, back, left and right. This is achieved by altering the pitch of each blade in a cyclic variation: increasing lift in one sector and simultaneously decreasing lift in the directly opposing sector. In doing so this causes the rotor blades on one side of the disc to flap up and the corresponding opposite blades to flap down, thus effectively tilting the disc. This results in the direction of

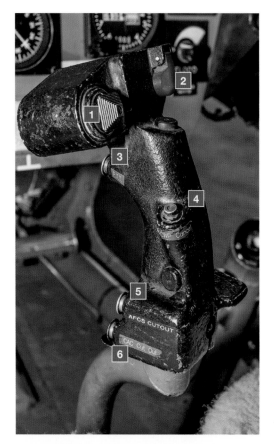

RIGHT The Pilot's cyclic stick.

1 Cyclic trim switch
2 Guarded external cargo-release button
3 Press to transmit
4 CWP cancel button
5 AFCS cut-out
6 CAC cut-out.

RIGHT The Pilot's collective lever.

1 Guarded jettison button
2 Landing light switch
3 Hydraulic servo switch
4 Rescue hoist control switch
5 Landing light directional switch
6 Collective channel-release button
7 Flotation bag manual operation button
8 Friction lock.

lift changing, causing the helicopter to alter direction in response.

In order to make these changes, cyclic sticks are positioned in front of the right-hand cockpit seat between the Pilot's knees. It is the adjustment of the cyclic stick which conveys inputs to control the fore, aft and lateral movement of the helicopter by altering the pitch of the main rotor blades individually. The handgrip at the top of the stick is fitted with switches and buttons to operate various systems, including the AFCS cut-out, cyclic trim and press-to-transmit radio button.

Collective control

While use of the cyclic stick to tilt the rotor disc will produce a change in direction of the lift force to effect directional changes, in order to generate and control lift, all four of the Lynx's main rotor blades need to be increased or decreased simultaneously and by the same amount. This is called collective control.

To do this a collective lever is situated to the left-hand side of the Pilot's seat (or both seats if the aircraft is configured as a dual-control version). As with the cyclic stick, the handgrip on the top of the Pilot's collective lever contains switches and buttons for underslung load jettison, landing light control, deck lock harpoon operation, flotation system, rescue hoist control and collective AFCS channel release to be operated conveniently. Although the positioning of these buttons reduces the need for the Pilot to take his hands off the controls, should it be necessary, a friction collar device is fitted to allow the lever's position to be maintained hands-free.

In the event of an emergency, such as engine failure, the aircraft can enter what is known as 'autorotation'. By lowering the collective lever fully to reduce pitch on the main rotor blades the aircraft will begin to descend rapidly. As it does so, air flows up through the main rotor disc causing the blades to continue rotating. At a pre-determined height, the Pilot will flare the aircraft to reduce forward speed by pulling back on the cyclic stick.

Doing so, however, will actually cause the main rotor speed (known as Nr) to begin to rise. To contain this increase and thereby prevent damage that would otherwise be caused by the main rotor overspeeding, the Pilot must carefully use small amounts of collective lever inputs. The increase in pitch angle of the main rotor blades will generate increased drag, helping to counter this speed increase.

Too much collective input will induce a greater amount of drag than is necessary to control the Nr, causing a rapid decay in the kinetic energy stored up in the rotor system and slowing the blades to a point at which they no longer generate any lift, whereupon the helicopter will simply fall out of the sky.

Maintaining this fine balancing act between Nr, lift and gravity will enable the rate of descent to be controlled until the helicopter is within approximately 10ft of the ground, whereupon the Pilot can progressively raise the collective lever all the way up, sacrificing all of the remaining Nr energy to generate a final amount of lift sufficient to help cushion the landing.

Collective interlinks

Operation of the collective lever can, however, produce unwanted aerodynamic effects. For instance, raising the collective results in the nose of the aircraft naturally rising, causing it to reduce airspeed. To reduce these effects, mechanical 'interlinks' consisting of a spring box and set of levers and cranks are fitted beneath the cockpit floor. These combine the collective inputs with other controls to change the effect on the aircraft.

The collective-to-fore/aft interlink beneath the cockpit floor automatically applies an amount of nose-down cyclic movement to compensate for this nose-up movement. Conversely, lowering the collective causes the nose to drop which is countered by the interlink automatically generating a backwards cyclic input to bring the nose back up again.

Likewise, altering the collective input changes the main rotor torque effect, causing the aircraft to yaw. Increasing the input makes the nose yaw to the right, while decreasing results in a yaw to the left.

A collective-yaw interlink is installed within the collective lever mechanism above the cockpit floor to the left-hand side of the Observer's seat. This increases the tail rotor pitch when the collective lever is raised, and reduces it when it is lowered.

Main rotor actuators

Although early helicopters were simple and light enough to be flown with manual flying controls, the effort needed to overcome the aerodynamic forces on the main and tail rotor blades to effect any manoeuvring nonetheless made it at best a tiring experience.

To relieve the Pilot of this strenuous task, all but the most basic of helicopters these days have hydraulically assisted powered flying controls. Unlike most of the older helicopters, however, the Lynx has no manual reversion option should the hydraulic systems fail. No hydraulics, no control.

First, inputs from the Pilot's collective, cyclic and yaw controls are transmitted mechanically via a series of flying control push/pull rods, levers and bellcranks from the cockpit to hydraulic control valves on each of the three independent MRAs fitted to the front face of the main rotor gearbox. In conjunction with the AFCS, these MRAs, powered by the Number 1 and Number 2 hydraulic systems, work in unison to translate the inputs from the Pilot's controls to outputs controlling the collective, fore and aft (pitch) and lateral (roll) movements to the main rotor head.

As the control valves are operated, so the MRA ram mounted to the MRGB begins to extend or retract, dependent upon the input, causing the entire MRA body to move up or down. The movement of the whole MRA body instead of just the actuating ram might seem odd at first, but in this way the body effectively

BELOW The cyclic lateral main rotor actuator (MRA) on the port side of the MRGB.

'catches up' with and reduces the input acting on the control valve. Once it reaches the point at which the input and outputs are the same – in other words the Pilot has stopped moving the controls – it effectively re-establishes a new datum and ceases until such time as it senses a change in the input again. This use of a datum and the sensing of a difference in the system is the means by which control is maintained. All three of the MRAs are connected to a beam lever mounted beneath the MRGB, which is itself attached via a knuckle joint to the bottom of the main rotor head spindle. The operation of this is described in the section entitled 'Main rotor head'.

Movements of the collective lever can, however, have a natural adverse effect on the aircraft in both the cyclic and yaw planes. Raising the lever, for instance, causes a nose-up pitching moment as well as altering the main rotor torque, which can affect directional stability.

Yaw control

Abiding by Sir Isaac Newton's third Law of Motion – which states that for every action there is an equal and opposite reaction – with the main rotor spinning in one direction and generating torque the fuselage suspended beneath will naturally try to rotate in the opposite direction and cause loss of directional control. To counteract and control this reactionary force, a vertically mounted anti-torque tail rotor is installed at the upper end of the tail pylon.

Unlike the main rotor blades, however, the tail rotor blades can only be altered collectively in pitch via foot-operated tail rotor pedals protruding through the cockpit floor in the Pilot's footwell. Each pedal moves through a set of brushes to prevent any loose objects from falling into the control run and jamming the pedals. Moving the left pedal forward will increase tail rotor pitch and cause the aircraft to yaw to the left; application of the right pedal will decrease the tail rotor pitch, reducing the thrust and allowing the natural torque reaction of the anti-clockwise rotating main rotor to make the aircraft turn to the right.

These pedals are adjustable fore and aft to suit the Pilot's leg length and, on dual-control-configured aircraft, are interconnected with each other to allow operation by the occupant of either seat.

The Pilot's inputs at the tail rotor pedals operate a series of push/pull rods and levers beneath the cabin floor to a quadrant on the left-hand side. At this quadrant the control is transferred to a set of braided steel flying control cables – six in total – linked in series via adjustable turnbuckles which allow the tension to be altered as required during the rigging of the flying control system.

Continuing this type of control right through to the tail rotor gearbox would not be a problem were it not for the folding tail pylon. This effectively causes a break in the tail rotor control system. To prevent having to disconnect cables and then have to reconnect and re-rig the whole system, the cables are attached to a cable tension regular quadrant assembly at the aft end of the tailcone. A set of tappets fixed within the tailcone impinge on a corresponding rocker assembly in the tail pylon. As the cable tension regulator is moved by the cables, so the inputs are transferred via the rocker assembly to a push/pull rod running up to the tail rotor servo mounted on the top of the tail rotor gearbox. The servo itself is connected to the gearbox by a pitch control arm which, when moved by the servo output, operates the pitch control level within the gearbox.

This in turn pushes/pulls against the pitch control beam at the end of which four pitch control rods are fitted. As these offset pitch change rods move, they cause the tail rotor

BELOW The Pilot's yaw pedals protruding through their protective brush assemblies. Here they are held in place by ground locks with the right pedal fully forward to offload the spring bias unit. To the left is the knob for adjusting the fore and aft positions of the pedals to allow for Pilots of different heights to reach the pedals comfortably.

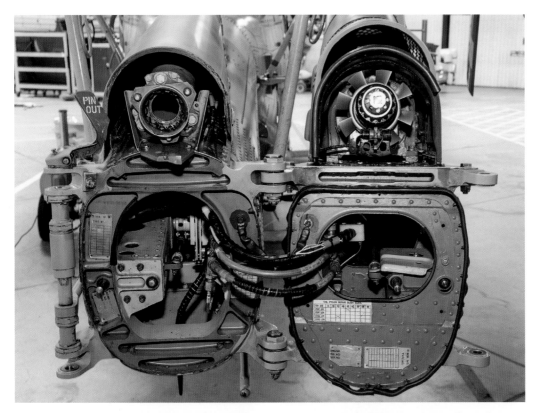

LEFT The aft end of the tailcone (left) with the cable tension regulator (light grey) just visible and the tappet assemblies. Electrical cables and hydraulic lines run between the two.

FAR LEFT Tappet assemblies on the tail cone which mate with …

LEFT … corresponding tappet assemblies on the tail pylon to allow the yaw control system to remain unaffected by folding and spreading of the tail.

blade sleeves to rotate around their axes, thus altering the pitch on each blade equally and simultaneously. It is this change in blade pitch that increases and decreases the effectiveness of the tail rotor to generate thrust in order to counteract the torque generated by the main rotor. In doing so, it provides the Pilot control over the direction in which the helicopter is pointing.

RIGHT The retaining spigot (visible above the letter 'D') that engages with a clip on the tailcone to secure the tail pylon when folded. The hinge area is given some environmental protection by a rubber seal.

Automatic flying control system (AFCS)

The Lynx uses a Mk.34 AFCS. Autostabilising Equipment (ASE) works by taking data from two vertical reference gyros fitted in the aft equipment bay, signals from two electrical pick-offs on the Pilot's cyclic stick and the aircraft's compass to control outputs to the MRAs. This maintains the attitude and heading of the aircraft at the point at which the system is engaged by the Pilot.

Hydraulic system

Aerodynamic and physical forces acting on the flying controls of helicopters can be extremely high, making control of the aircraft difficult, tiring and often impossible. To help to overcome these forces and achieve almost effortless control, the main and tail rotors are controlled by hydraulic actuators that amplify small input movements into large output forces.

The Lynx has two main hydraulic systems: Number 1 and Number 2. Both of these systems provide hydraulic power to the MRAs fitted to the front of the MRGB and can do so

independently of each other should one fail. However, the Number 1 system also provides hydraulic power to the tail rotor servo control unit. Unlike the main rotor system, the tail rotor can revert to manual control, assisted by the spring bias unit. If both Number 1 and Number 2 systems fail together, however, the Pilot will lose control of the aircraft.

A third – Number 3 – system provides services for utility, non-essential items such as the winch, deck harpoon and wheel brakes. It shares its fluid supply with the Number 1 system reservoir.

The main components of the hydraulic systems are situated on aluminium alloy manifold assemblies mounted on the cabin roof in front of the MRGB on either side: Number 1 and 3 systems on the left and Number 2 system on the right.

For the Number 1 and Number 2 systems, a variable output nine-cylinder ABEX (Air Brake Extreme) hydraulic pump is mounted on and driven by the accessory gearbox of the MRGB, drawing OM-15 hydraulic fluid from the large blue-painted 6.82-litre reservoirs on the manifold assemblies and pumping it at $2{,}000\text{lbf/in}^2$

BELOW Viewed from the port side, the area immediately in front of the MRGB shows the blue-painted Numbers 1 and 3 hydraulic system reservoir and the white-covered cyclic lateral MRA. Behind can be seen the Number 1 alternator, which is driven by the MRGB.

1 AC generator cooling ducting
2 Numbers 1 and 3 hydraulic system reservoir
3 Reservoir filter blockage pop-up indicator
4 Number 1 AC generator
5 Cyclic lateral control rod
6 Cyclic lateral MRA servo valve actuator linkage
7 Cyclic lateral MRA.

and up to 17.3litre/min via a filter, pressure sensor, accumulator and pressure switch to the MRAs. These reservoirs have small pop-up filter blockage indicators which activate when a blockage is detected in the system pressure.

Number 3 system is driven by a variable seven-cylinder NYAB (New York Air Brake) pump fitted on and driven by the Number 1 engine auxiliary gearbox, providing 2,030lbf/in^2 of pressure.

A hydraulic accumulator holds a small amount of fluid and, using an air/nitrogen charge acting against a piston, dampens out pulsations generated by the pumps and compensates for any fluctuations in system pressure caused by control movement.

Fuel system

The Lynx fuel system comprises five separate but interconnected flexible self-sealing bag-type tanks with a total capacity of between 1,161lb (802kg) and 1,139lb (780kg) depending upon whether gravity or pressure refuelling is used; a forward tank and separate port and starboard collector tanks are situated beneath the cabin floor. The port and starboard main tanks are positioned behind the rear cabin bulkhead above the floor level. A single pressure refuelling coupling point is found on the starboard side of the rear fuselage under a flap behind the sponson, which allows the system to be pressure refuelled or suction defuelled.

The forward tank transfers fuel into both port and starboard collector tanks proportionally. Under normal conditions the port main and port collector tank group supply fuel to the Number 1 engine. Similarly the starboard main and starboard collector tank group supply the Number 2 engine. Under emergency conditions, however, either engine can be fed from one group or one engine from both groups.

Contents units within each tank send an electrical signal to a single contents gauge in the cockpit to display the amount of fuel contained within the tanks. A rotary switch in the cockpit allows the contents of the port, starboard and forward tanks to be displayed individually as well as a 'Total' selection where the contents of all of the tanks are added together.

Main tanks

The port and starboard main tanks occupy spaces behind the cabin rear bulkhead. Both have a capacity of 469lb (213kg) when pressure refuelled or 445lb (202kg) under gravity refuelling conditions for which each has its own gravity filler cap.

High-level float switches automatically close the refuel/defuel valve when the tanks are full. All of the fuel tanks have air vents to prevent damage occurring through pressure build-up within the system. These vents feed into the main tanks. The main tanks then vent through pipes to the underside of the aircraft. If over-fuelling occurs, fuel will be forced through these vents to atmosphere to prevent any damage to the system. Special valves prevent the system from continuing to syphon once the fuelling has stopped.

Fuel flows under gravity from the main tanks into their respective collector tanks. When the contents drop below the one-third level, float switches operate the transfer pumps in the forward tank to begin the transfer of fuel into the collector tanks. In this way, the aircraft's centre of gravity (CofG) is maintained within safe levels. Jettison valves fitted within the main tanks allow fuel to be dumped in an emergency situation.

Forward tank

The forward fuel tank is installed beneath the cabin floor and has a capacity of 344lb (156kg). It contains two transfer pumps to allow fuel to be pumped into each of the collector tanks in order to maintain the aircraft's CofG. If the fuel runs low, a low-level shut-off switch operates to stop the transfer pumps and prevent them from overheating. A fuel and a water drain allow gravity draining of fuel and sampling to check for the presence of water.

Collector tanks

The port and starboard collector tanks are installed beneath the cabin floor aft of the forward tank; each has a capacity of 242lb (110kg). As the name implies, the collector tanks take fuel from the forward and main tanks in preparation for pumping to the fuel manifold. Under normal operation, the port main and port collector tanks supply fuel to the Number 1 engine while the starboard main and starboard

RIGHT A pair of overload tanks, carrying up to 359lb of additional fuel, that can be mounted in the cabin in lieu of the seats and plumbed into the fuel system for increased range.

RIGHT The pressure refuelling point and controls are situated on the rear fuselage starboard side under a quick-release flap, upon which are details of the approved fuels for both normal and emergency use.

BELOW A Lynx Observer assisting with the rotors-running pressure refuel of a Lynx on board HMS *Bulwark*. *(LA(Phot) Joel Rouse/Crown Copyright)*

collector tanks supply the Number 2 engine. Fuel is transferred from the forward tank into both collector tanks equally and from the main tanks under gravity to their respective collector tanks. As with the forward tank, the collector tanks have a water drain that can be used to gravity-drain the fuel from the system.

The tanks have a DC-supplied, AC-driven booster pump to transfer fuel through to the fuel low pressure (LP) manifold, a contents unit, and a float-type low-level switch which sends a signal to illuminate the 'Fuel Low' caption on the cockpit CWP when the fuel remaining drops to 103lb (47kg) to warn the Pilot that approximately 20 minutes' worth of fuel remains.

Overload tanks

An aluminium alloy overload tank, capable of carrying up to 791lb (359kg) of extra fuel to extend the range of the aircraft, can be fitted in the far aft of the cabin on quick-release mounts. This would be where the three-man troop seat would normally fit and is connected into the main fuel system via a coupling on the cabin deck. It can also be carried to increase the aircraft's AUM for training purposes. Although the tank has its own built-in fuel gauge, it is not visible from the cockpit.

Fuel supply to engines

Installed within a fuel-proof bag on the forward bulkhead in the aft equipment bay is a fuel manifold assembly which takes the fuel pumped from the port and starboard collector tank booster pumps and supplies it to the Number 1 and Number 2 engines. It comprises two electrically operated LP cocks – one for each engine – to isolate the fuel supply, pressure switches to give cockpit indication of booster pump operation and an electrically operated cross-feed cock to allow fuel delivery to be diverted from one side of the system to feed the opposite engine in an emergency. Non-return valves prevent return flow of fuel if cross-feed is selected.

Refuelling, defuelling and jettisoning

The Lynx is normally pressure refuelled as it is quicker, with a flow rate of 815lb/min (370kg/min) at a pressure of 55psi, as well as being safer (atomised fuel vapour cannot escape and pose a fire hazard, especially during rotors-running refuel) because it does not allow as much fuel to be carried. A standard NATO refuel coupling is situated on the starboard side of the rear fuselage under a spring-loaded flap underneath the starboard engine exhaust. Alongside the coupling, which is protected by a cap held on by a metal chain, is a refuel/defuel switch, a defuel valve position magnetic indicator and a 'tanks full' light.

With the refuel/defuel valves selected to open, fuel begins to flow under pressure into the collector tanks. As these become full, the increased pressure forces fuel up through the open-bore pipes into the main tanks. As the level reaches the one-third stack pipe level, fuel flows down these pipes to the forward tank and, if fitted, to the auxiliary overload tank.

Once the high-level float switch in the main tanks is activated, the 'tanks full' light illuminates and the defuel/refuel valve is shut off, stopping any further fuel from flowing.

The contents of all of the fuel tanks, including the auxiliary overload tank if fitted, can be pressure defuelled by suction through the refuel coupling at 11psi or by gravity through drain valves in the bottom of the forward and collector tanks. In an emergency, a guarded switch on the fuel management panel in the cockpit, highlighted with black and yellow stripes, can be selected to 'OPEN'. This will open the jettison valves in the lower half of each main tank. Fuel will begin to flow at an average rate of 125lb/min (57kg/min) out of a jettison pipe fitted inboard of the port undercarriage sponson. As the level in the main tanks reaches the one-third point, the float switches will activate the transfer pumps in the forward tank. As the collector tanks are already full, the increased pressure will cause the excess fuel to be forced back up through stack pipes into the main tanks and eventually out to the atmosphere. Once the forward tank is empty, however, the pressure in the collector tanks reduces and, with no pump facility, the collector tank content can no longer be jettisoned. The main tanks continue to discharge until the jettison valves are switched off manually by the Pilot.

Landing gear

The requirement for the aircraft to land on a ship and be able to turn 360 degrees on deck (with rotors turning) on to whatever heading the wind was blowing from and, in doing so, negate the need for the ship to alter on to a specific flying course, led the Naval variant of

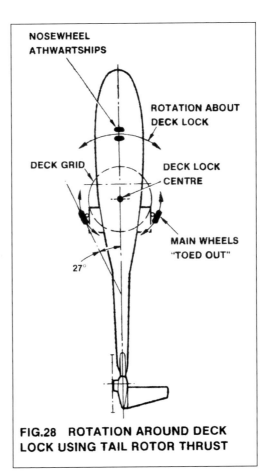

NOSEWHEEL ATHWARTSHIPS

ROTATION ABOUT DECK LOCK

DECK GRID

DECK LOCK CENTRE

MAIN WHEELS "TOED OUT"

27°

FIG.28 ROTATION AROUND DECK LOCK USING TAIL ROTOR THRUST

LEFT A diagram illustrating the use of the toed-out mainwheels, rotated nosewheel, deck lock harpoon and tail rotor thrust while embarked on a small ship's flight deck to enable the aircraft to turn on to any given heading. *(AgustaWestland)*

the Lynx to be designed with a three-unit, non-retractable, tricycle-arrangement undercarriage.

This ability to turn on the spot is achieved through the use of a combination of articulated and fixed oleo assemblies whose wheels are positioned on the circumference of an imaginary circle with the aircraft being held on deck by the deck lock (harpoon) assembly at its centre point.

Each unit is of a double air/nitrogen charge design, which allows for the absorption of greater landing loads without any structural damage to the aircraft and with minimal recoil – particularly necessary for a seagoing aircraft where pitching and rolling decks can often lead to heavier than normal landings. Having made a difficult approach to land on the back of a ship only to bounce off because the undercarriage cannot dampen out the forces is clearly not an attractive proposition! The oleos are also designed to maintain a 300mm (1ft) clearance between the underside of the aircraft and the ground or deck in order to prevent any damage occurring to weapons or stores that may be being carried.

Nose oleo

The nose oleo assembly is bolted on to the bulkhead on the aircraft's centreline below the cockpit floor. It comprises a shock absorber to damp out vertical loads, a castoring actuator to turn the assembly, twin nosewheels and wheel locks. Ordinarily held in the fore and aft positions by locks, the Pilot can, through selecting a hydraulic castoring actuator switch in the cockpit, rotate the nose oleo and wheels through 90 degrees to the right. In this configuration, and by operating the yaw pedals, the tail rotor thrust can be used to swivel the aircraft through 360 degrees.

Main oleos and sponsons

Single mainwheels are mounted on to oleos bolted on the outboard frames of the port and starboard sponson assemblies. These oleo units are identical and therefore can be interchanged. Ordinarily they are angled (toed out) at 27.5 degrees, to allow the aircraft to rotate on the spot when the nose oleo is at 90 degrees to the fore and aft positions. In the event of a tail rotor failure where a run-on landing is required to minimise torque effect from the main rotor, the friction that they generate as they are scuffed along the ground effectively provides a rudimentary braking system to slow the aircraft down.

ABOVE The twin nosewheel assembly with the wheel lock manual-release levers in between.

RIGHT The port main undercarriage with wheel orientated fore and aft for towing. Blue wheel brake hoses curl around the outside of the scissor link, which prevents the wheel from rotating around the oleo axis. In its compressed state, the oleo extension protrudes through a hole in the upper fairing.

Wheels

Both the twin nosewheels and single mainwheels are of split hub construction. The nosewheels measure 13½in × 4¼in, while the mainwheels are 18in × 5½in. Both have tyres with inner tubes.

The twin mainwheels have locking assemblies made from a toothed inner face to the wheel rim, into which engage a spring-loaded toothed plunger. This plunger can be operated under hydraulic pressure or manually (for ground handling when electrical and hydraulic power is not connected) by way of a small handle located on the inboard aft side of each wheel.

A spring-loaded ground lock pin must be withdrawn before the aircraft is towed on the ground, otherwise damage will occur – expensive and embarrassing!

RIGHT To manoeuvre the aircraft on the ground while ashore, a towing arm attached to a tractor is used. A handle is turned to operate a set of jaws, forcing pins to engage with the axle ends.

Rescue hoist

An electrically controlled hydraulically operated rescue hoist can be fitted in the cabin on the starboard side. The jib is supported by a main load-bearing strut and can be slewed in for stowage and out for use by pulling on a slew lock release inside and above the cabin door and then manually turning a handwheel which operates a screw actuator strut. It is capable of lifting and lowering a maximum load of 600lb (272kg) and has a cable length of 100ft. There are two different operating positions dependent upon whether the starboard stores carrier is fitted or not.

Hydraulic power for the hoist comes from the Number 3 hydraulic system. It can be electrically controlled from a three-position switch on the Pilot's collective lever or from a three-position switch situated above the starboard cabin door.

In the event of the hoist cable becoming jammed, or in an emergency, the Pilot or Winchman can press a jettison button to cut the cable using a cartridge-operated cable-cutter through which the cable passes.

The hoist can also be used for fast roping to enable a boarding party to be deployed to vessels by rope when the aircraft is otherwise unable to land. Ropes up to 90ft in length can

RIGHT The rescue hoist is fitted on the starboard side of the cabin and is stowed internally when not in use.

1 To unlock the hoist and allow it to be swung out of the open cabin door, a release cord just inside the cabin roof is pulled.

2 A wheel is turned which operates a screw jack to extend the jib of the hoist.

3 The hoist is then manually swung out and locked into position.

4 The jib of the hoist in the fully extended position ready for use.

be attached directly to the hoist hook or via a quick-release mechanism (QRM).

Deck lock

Landing on a pitching, rolling deck – especially at the stern of a ship where the pitching moment is greatest – gives rise to the potential for any aircraft to suddenly be thrown off and end up overboard. Employing some method of immediately anchoring an aircraft to the deck before the deck party can apply their nylon lashings is therefore very desirable.

A telescopic, hydraulically powered harpoon is fitted in its own bay on the centerline of the aircraft between the main undercarriage. On contact with the ship's deck, the Pilot operates the harpoon by a switch on the collective lever. Powered by the Number 3 hydraulic system, the harpoon is normally held in the retracted position by hydraulic pressure. When selected, pressure is applied to the extend-side of the hydraulic ram, causing it to extend up to 10.82in (275mm) until the head passes through the deck lock grid on the flight deck and the spring-loaded locking jaws close. When this happens, the extension pressure being applied is stopped and the harpoon automatically begins to retract, pulling the aircraft down on to the grid and holding it securely in position. A shear pin is added for safety, breaking when the force upon it exceeds 8,000lb (3,628kg).

If the head fails to find one of the holes in the grid, the harpoon body will be deflected off the deck at an angle. When this exceeds 15 degrees, a microswitch releases the pressure causing the ram to extend, and allowing the head to retract again, recentre and extend once more, hopefully finding its target this time.

The harpoon head is designed so that it is free to turn through 360 degrees, allowing the aircraft to turn on the deck while still firmly attached.

SACRU

An electrically operated Semi-Automatic Cargo Release Unit (SACRU) is fitted beneath the aircraft to allow it to carry external loads weighing up to 3,000lb (1,360kg). With underslung loads the aircraft is restricted to flying at a maximum of 60 knots. Usually held securely against the belly of the aircraft by a bungee cord when not in use, the SACRU has a large hook on to which load-lifting strop equipment can be attached. These strops are then held securely in place with a spring-loaded keeper plate that can be opened via an electrical solenoid operated from a switch on the Pilot's cyclic stick.

In an emergency, a guarded button on the Pilot's collective lever can be pressed, causing the hook to open and the underslung load to be jettisoned.

Electrical system

The Lynx HMA Mk.8's electrical power is provided by three separate built-in systems: a battery, a DC generation system and an AC generation system.

Fitted in the aft equipment bay is a large nickel–cadmium battery providing 24-volt, 23-ampere-hour, connected to the battery bus bar. By selecting the battery master switch to 'ON', this bus bar is connected to the essential bus bar to supply the aircraft's vital flight systems; its use is limited primarily to ground operations when external power is not available and as a source of emergency power in the event of generator failure. If a DC ground supply is connected to the aircraft, the battery is automatically deselected.

Both of the aircraft's Gem engines have,

mounted on their accessory gearboxes, their own dual-purpose DC starter/generator units. As the name suggests, they can be used as starter motors to turn the engine during the start sequence, after which they become driven by the engine to provide 28-volt 6kW power via the DC general bus bar to the essential bus bar. Just one of these starter/generators is capable of supplying the entire aircraft's DC power requirements in the event of an engine failure.

During ground servicing and engine starts a 28-volt DC supply can be plugged into the aircraft via a three-pin connector fitted beneath a flap on the left-hand side of the fuselage aft of the undercarriage sponson.

Fitted to and powered by the MRGB are two AC alternators, each producing 15-kVA at

LEFT The hydraulic deck lock harpoon in its stowed position. The head is covered in grease to protect it from salt water damage.

LEFT The Semi-Automatic Cargo Release Unit (SACRU) mounted on the belly and held in the stowed position with a bungee cord.

BELOW The 24-volt, 23-ampere-hour nickel–cadmium battery installed just inside the aft equipment bay in between the two flotation bottles.

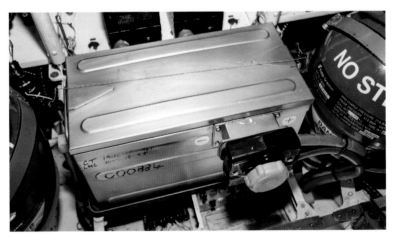

ABOVE A 28V DC ground power unit plugged into the sockets on the rear fuselage ready for engine start.

gearbox fairing. All three lamps can be set to steady or flashing modes to give signals to the FDO and crew during night deck operations.

Anti-collision lights

An Oxley dual red and infrared high-intensity strobe light (HISL) is fitted on the upper tail rotor gearbox fairing. Two xenon flash tubes – one red and one white – will flash intermittently to make the aircraft more conspicuous to any nearby aircraft. The infrared (IR) light is invisible to the naked eye.

Search and landing lamp

An IR/white retractable, adjustable, dual-mode search and landing lamp is installed in the belly of the aircraft. Controlled by a switch on the Pilot's collective lever, the lamp can be adjusted through 90 degrees from the housed position and then rotated through 360 degrees clockwise and anti-clockwise. While the lamp can be turned off in any position, selecting the switch to retract causes the lamp to automatically return to its housed position whereupon the light extinguishes.

Downward identification light

A downward identification light is fitted on the belly of the aircraft and can be switched on or operated in a Morse configuration as a signal lamp, being used as such during deck operations at night to signal the Pilot's intentions to the deck party.

Infrared formation lights

Tiny *Starpoint* formation lights are mounted on small brackets on the outside of the cockpit and underneath the tailcone near the tail fold. These emit infrared light that allows Pilots to determine

115/200 volts. These come on line when the Number 1 engine is in accessory drive. An AC ground-power supply can be plugged in via a six-pin connector on the rear fuselage directly beneath the DC ground supply plug.

Lighting

The Lynx is fitted with a series of external lights and lamps that serve as a safety measure to aid the aircraft's visibility, as a means of communication between aircrew and the Flight Deck Officer (FDO) during night operations and also help to illuminate landing areas.

Navigation lights

Three coloured lamps are fitted to the aircraft to show its direction of travel to other aircraft in poor weather and at night. A red lamp is installed on the left-hand cockpit footstep, a green one on the starboard cockpit footstep and a white one at the aft end of the tail rotor

RIGHT The rear navigation light at the aft end of the tail rotor gearbox cowling.

FAR RIGHT The upper HISL anti-collision beacon.

ABOVE The starboard forward *Starpoint* IR formation light fitted on the Pilot's cockpit door.

ABOVE The aft *Starpoint* IR formation lights fitted on a bracket beneath the tailcone near the tail pylon fold. Immediately aft is the IFF aerial.

LEFT The *Seaspray 3030* radar scanner fitted beneath the nose, seen here with protective radome removed.

the position of an aircraft while in formation and while using NVDs.

Surveillance systems

Radar

The Lynx HMA Mk.8 is fitted with a *Seaspray* 3030 180-degree radar with a scanner mounted ventrally beneath the cockpit and surrounded by a protective glass-reinforced plastic radome. It can detect and track small, fast surface vessels, interrogate I-band transponders fitted to aircraft or shipping and provide data to the *Sea Skua* missile system for target location and homing.

Central Tactical System

The CTS is the 'fighting heart' of the Lynx. It maintains control over the communications, GPS navigation, radar, ESM, tactical data and stores management system and integrates and processes data from them all to provide the Observer with tactical and navigational information displayed on the Tactical Situation Display – Graphics (TSD-G) screen in the cockpit. The CTS is primarily controlled via the two CDNUs in the interseat console, comprising a keyboard and display screen. Data can be inputted manually and overlaid on to video being fed to the TSD-G display from the PID and radar.

LEFT The TSD-G displaying navigational data.

ESM

The Lynx is fitted with *Orange Crop* ESM, used to passively detect, identify and locate the radars of other aircraft and vessels without giving the aircraft's position away. There are a total of six aerials on the aircraft: two on the nose structure, one on each of the two sponsons and one either side of the rear fuselage. The ESM controller is positioned above the main instrument panel in the cockpit. Data is processed by the CTS and displayed on the TSD-G and CDNUs.

PID

The GEC-Marconi *Sea Owl* PID, mounted in a steerable gyro-stabilised turret on the nose of the aircraft, combines a thermal imaging sensor with a telescope, capable of ×5 and ×30 magnification, to allow the Lynx to conduct long-range surveillance and identification of surface ship targets, outside of the range of enemy weapons.

The sensor itself is protected by an optically flat germanium IR window with a hard carbon coating capable of withstanding bird-strikes. A small windscreen wiper and washer fluid contained in a tank in the nose allows the window to be cleaned in flight. A brake system allows the turret to remain steady in any given position and when not in use, it is rotated to point aft to protect the window.

ABOVE The two black *Orange Crop* ESM aerials on the nose of the aircraft.

RIGHT The *Sea Owl* PID turret showing the optically flat germanium IR window. The PID is seen here removed from the aircraft for servicing.

RIGHT The eerie green image produced by the PID displayed on the TSD-G, here showing the Flight's personnel conducting a 'FOD plod' (foreign object damage) on the flight deck and hangar roof of HMS *Monmouth* prior to recovery of the Lynx.

**LEFT Lower fuselage
aerials:**

1 Forward UHF SATURN aerial
2 VHF AIS antenna
3 Bowman VHF radio aerial
4 Downward identification light
5 Doppler aerial.

IR radiation is given off naturally by any object with a temperature above absolute zero (−273°C). In order to produce strong enough signals from which highly sensitive IR images can be generated, a Jules-Thompson mini compressor unit in the nose of the aircraft cools the PID's built-in detector unit down to this cryogenic temperature. Data from the aircraft's CTS is fed into the PID to allow the turret to be directed on to any given azimuth and elevation angle and lock on to a particular target regardless of the aircraft's attitude.

Communications systems

The Lynx HMA Mk.8 has a series of communication systems used for different purposes. From the Collins 718U-5 HF radio, through Airterm KY100 wideband secure speech, *Bowman* VHF, VHF/UHF and AD3400 UHF radios to the simplest of communication methods – the ARI1802 telebrief cable – the Lynx is well equipped.

Transponder
The Lynx has a Pilkington ARI 5983 I-Band transponder using an aerial under the tailcone and one on the extreme nose between the two ESM aerials. There is also a SIFF Mk.XII transponder providing automatic radar identification to other airborne or ground stations when interrogated. IFF aerials are positioned one on the forward fuselage and another under the tailcone.

Bowman VHF radio
The Lynx HMA Mk.8 is fitted with *Bowman* VHF radio, allowing the aircraft to communicate with land and amphibious units during operations.

Collins 718U-5 HF radio
The Lynx has a Collins 718U-5 HF radio with associated antennae, consisting of a wire aerial running between two masts and a monopole aerial on the starboard underside of the aft equipment bay.

**BELOW The forward
UHF and homing
aerials on the
nose. Temporarily
fitted behind them
is a special data
acquisition unit
camera used for
optical tracking of the
main rotor blades.**

RIGHT The GPS aerial mounted in the fixed tail rotor driveshaft (TRDS) tunnel fairing.

Talon V/UHF radio

Talon RT-8106 is a V/UHF secure communications radio incorporating SATURN. It integrates with the KY100 air terminals housed in the aft equipment bay and utilises an aerial underneath the tailcone.

SATURN

The Second Generation Anti-Jam Tactical UHF Radio for NATO (SATURN) allows the aircraft to transmit and receive communications with the surface fleet by being made more difficult for enemy forces to jam through the employment of so-called 'frequency hopping' cryptographic technology. The system is programmed with specific cryptographic data on a daily basis, allowing the system to encode the transmissions.

Weaponry

The Lynx HMA Mk.8 is capable of carrying a range of different types of weaponry including an M3M machine gun, *Stingray* torpedoes, depth charges and *Sea Skua* missiles.

M3M machine gun

The FN Herstal 0.5in M3M is a fearsome weapon. Fully automated and recoil-operated, this heavy machine gun packs a mighty punch with its 12.7mm rounds which come in 100-round boxes or in a 600-round cradle, including armour-piercing, tracer and ball types.

The 100-round box is fitted to the side of the pintle head assembly while the much larger 600-round cradle is attached to the cabin floor with ammunition being fed to the gun via a flexible feed chute containing 95 links. Links from expended rounds of ammunition are caught in a collection basket at the base of the pintle, preventing them from becoming a hazard to the aircraft.

The gun can be fitted in the cabin on the port or starboard sides on its own carrier and is used by either the Observer or a dedicated Air

ABOVE Staring down the barrel: Lieutenant Commander Alex Sims, RN, briefs Observer Lieutenant Mark Finnie, RN, on the use of the M3M gun prior to a live gunnery exercise. A 600-round magazine is fitted with rounds being fed along a flexible link.

RIGHT The 600-round magazine with flexible feed link mounted in the rear cabin.

OPPOSITE A Lynx HMA Mk.8 fitted with M3M gun on the starboard weapon carrier and a single *Stingray* torpedo on the port carrier.

ANATOMY OF THE LYNX HMA MK.8

RIGHT **RIGHT** For the purpose of this exercise, boxes of 100 rounds are being used, seen here being prepared for loading.

BELOW Taking aim through the laser rangefinder, spent cartridges spew out of the side as the M3M blasts away.

BOTTOM Tracer rounds from the M3M gun hitting the water.

Door Gunner to provide airborne firepower in air-to-air or air-to-surface scenarios.

Sea Skua

The Lynx HMA Mk.8 is capable of carrying up to four British Aerospace *Sea Skua* air-to-surface anti-shipping missiles mounted on external weapon carriers fitted to lugs adjacent to the cabin doors on both sides. The missiles, which weigh 330lb (150kg) each, have a flight time of between 75 and 125 seconds, by which stage they can achieve a range of up to about 15 miles flying at very high subsonic speeds. The Lynx's Observer can 'paint' the chosen target using the *Seaspray* radar with the missiles homing head being attracted to the reflected radar energy. Upon hitting the target, the missile is designed to penetrate the vessel's hull before exploding the 61lb (28kg) blast fragmentation warhead to cause maximum damage.

Sea Skua was first tested from a Lynx HAS Mk.2 on the firing ranges at Aberporth in 1981 and eight were fired during Operation Corporate in the Falklands the following year: four from Lynx flying from HMS *Coventry* and HMS *Glasgow*, and a further four against a cargo ship and a patrol boat.

During the 1991 Gulf War, Lynx from HMS

BELOW A *Sea Skua* inert round is prepared in the ship's hangar for loading on to the aircraft. As with anything on board, the cradle assembly must be lashed to the deck to prevent it from moving inadvertently.

Cardiff and HMS Gloucester fired a total of 12 Sea Skuas against Iraqi fast patrol boats off Kuwait. Lynx HAS.3GMS XZ230 of 214 Flight HMS Cardiff is credited not only with firing the first Sea Skua of the war, but the most in anger of any Lynx: a total of 7. Meanwhile, XZ720 of 216 Flight HMS Gloucester is credited with firing a total of 5.

Stingray

The Lynx is capable of carrying up to two BAeS Stingray lightweight anti-submarine torpedoes, which have a range of about 6 miles (10km).

Depth charge Mk.11

The Lynx can also carry up to two Mk.11 depth charges on the weapon carriers.

Defensive Aid Suite

Being able to engage with an enemy target and deliver the decisive blow first is of course the

ABOVE Two inert *Stingray* torpedo practice rounds on their trolleys. The pod at the rear (left) contains the parachute assembly.

BELOW Firing off M147 flares during a demonstration.

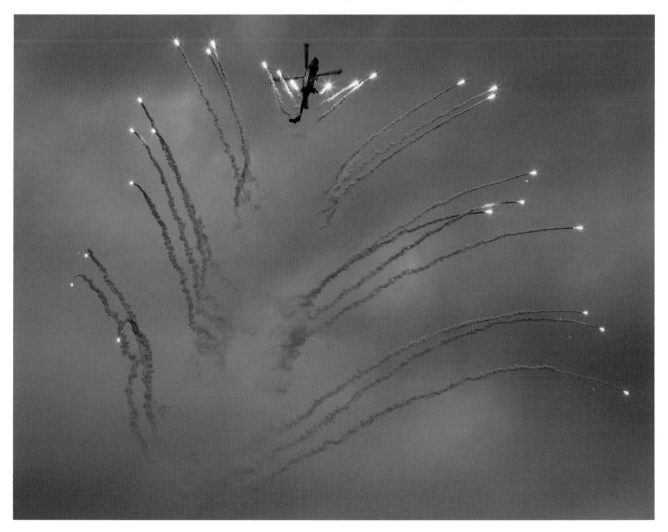

RIGHT The starboard rear EOMS and HF aerial.

RIGHT The starboard forward flare dispenser (minus cartridge) fitted beneath the undercarriage sponson.

RIGHT The IRCM jammer fitted on a turret immediately aft of the aft equipment bay door.

ultimate aim; but if in the process you become the target, then having the ability to detect any threat and deploy defensive countermeasures accordingly is naturally very important. To do this, the Lynx HMA Mk.8 has a Defensive Aid Suite (DAS) which comprises an AN/AAR 57 Common Missile Warning System.

Five passive electro-optic missile sensors (EOMS) mounted one on both sides of the nose, both sides of the rear fuselage and one on the belly of the aircraft, act as the aircraft's 'eyes' by detecting the launch of surface-to-air missiles (SAMs) via the ultraviolet radiation emissions from their exhaust plumes, giving audio warnings to the crew and a visual indication in the cockpit of the quadrant from which the threat is coming.

A firing signal will be sent automatically to the Joyce-Loebl M147 Countermeasures Dispensing System (CMDS) to fire off flares from the dispensers fitted beneath the undercarriage sponsons (and, depending on modification status, on top of the sponsons) in pre-determined patterns to fool the missile's heat-seeking detector head and cause it to lock on to a burning flare rather than the aircraft's own engine exhaust heat signature. Up to 120 flares can be carried.

Although capable of being entirely autonomous, the system can also be initiated manually by the crew.

A Sanders ALQ 144A (V) infrared jammer (IRJ) is fitted directly beneath the transportation joint on the rear fuselage, but is not integrated into the DAS system and operates independently. It generates a high-power IR light through a series of mirrored windows to jam the seeker head of IR-seeking missiles, confusing them and breaking their lock on to the aircraft.

Emergency equipment

Flotation bags

When helicopters are operated over large expanses of sea, the potential for engine failure leading to a ditching in the water is ever-present. In the event that such a situation

LEFT The port main flotation bag showing the space into which it fits in the undercarriage sponson structure.

occurs, the aircraft will almost inevitably capsize and quickly sink.

The Lynx is fitted with four inflatable bags to help to give the aircraft buoyancy in the event of it landing on the water and thereby afford the crew and any passengers more time to make their escape. Two bags are installed in the nose beneath the lower footstep windows. The bags take approximately 2–3 seconds to fully inflate when helium is forced into them under pressure. These nose bags measure 36in (914mm); two larger bags are fitted into recesses in the outer sections of the two main undercarriage sponsons, measuring 52in (1,320mm) when deployed.

The system is fully automatic – being activated by two submersion actuators – but if a fault develops they can be manually triggered by a switch on the Pilot's collective lever.

With all four bags inflated at maximum operating weight, the Lynx is designed to remain upright on the surface in a 15-degree nose-up attitude for approximately 10 minutes. In reality, inflation bags can often become damaged during ditching, especially into rough seas. Should the nose bags fail to operate or burst, the nose of the aircraft will sink in 35 seconds. If opposing nose and main bags fail, the aircraft will roll over after 20 seconds, becoming inverted after 5 seconds and will begin to sink after 30 seconds. Failure of a single main bag, however, causes the aircraft to capsize and begin to sink after just 12 seconds.

Life-raft

Should the aircraft end up in the sea, of course, a five-man life-raft is carried in the cabin, stowed in a bright yellow container in the left-hand seat along the rear bulkhead and secured by the five-point harness.

Crash-survivable cockpit voice recorder

Similar to modern airliners, the Lynx is now fitted with a crash-survivable cockpit voice recorder (CSCVR). Housed in an orange-painted box, the CSCVR is fitted under the Pilot's seat and has an integral sonar locating beacon to allow it to be tracked underwater. It records sounds from the radios, intercom and from ambient noise in the cockpit via a

LEFT The flotation bag unravelled. White French chalk is used to ease the packing process.

LEFT The port forward flotation bag assembly in the hinged-open position to allow access to control runs behind.

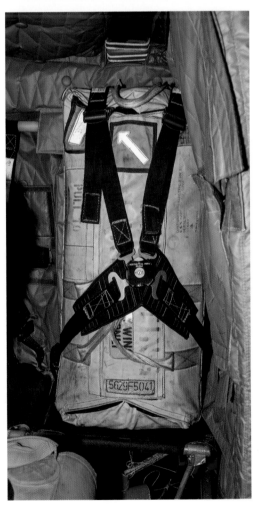

LEFT Securely stowed in a seating position with a five-point harness on the port side of the cabin is the MS-5 five-man life-raft.

RIGHT **The CSCVR fitted under the Pilot's seat (seen here with the seat removed).**

OPPOSITE **A view of the Number 1 engine installation.**

1 MRGB oil cooler matrix
2 Engine door locking pin
3 Centre firewall
4 Engine oil tank
5 Starter/generator cooling intake
6 Starter/generator
7 Starter/generator exhaust
8 Engine oil cooler intake
9 Engine oil cooler
10 Engine oil cooler exhaust
11 Engine auxiliary gearbox casing
12 Number 3 hydraulic system NYAB pump
13 Front firewall
14 Engine oil pipes in fireproof sheathing.

microphone on a 120-minute continuous loop. The recording stops 10 minutes after the oil pressure on both engines reduces below a certain level.

Engine – Rolls-Royce Gem Mk.204 and Mk.205

The Roll-Royce Gem turboshaft is a modular construction engine containing three independent, coaxially mounted main rotating assemblies: two 'spools' – a low pressure (LP) axial-flow spool; a high pressure (HP) centrifugal spool; and a free power turbine (FPT) and reduction gearbox. The engines are nominally identical to each other but the Number 1 engine becomes 'handed' when being prepared for installation by the fitting of a Number 3 system hydraulic pump.

By using two compressor types, each suited to different operating speed ranges, changes in power demands can be responded to much more quickly than other types of engine. Their independence from each other also allows them to operate within their own, most efficient speed bands at the same time.

LP spool

The LP spool consists of a four-stage axial-flow LP compressor to give high compression ratios but within a narrow rpm band. Each 'stage' is made up of fixed stator blades which direct airflow at the optimum angle on to adjacent rotor blades in order to cause them to turn. At the aft end of the hollow LP shaft is a single-stage LP turbine comprising fixed nozzles to guide the hot gases being generated by the combustion chamber on to rotating turbine blades. It is the turning of the turbine disc at the back, therefore, that drives the compressor at the front to feed the engine with air.

RIGHT **The Number 1 (left) and Number 2 Rolls-Royce Gem engines. On top of the titanium centre firewall can be seen the pin and T-handle that lock the upper doors in place.**

HP spool

Unlike the axial-flow LP spool, the HP spool is a single-stage centrifugal compressor driven by a single-stage HP turbine. This type of compressor, which helps to reduce the overall length and therefore the weight of the engine, produces significantly lower compression ratios but can operate in a much higher rpm band. It takes the form of an impeller and shroud with convergent ducts, which compresses and directs the airflow into the combustion chamber. The HP spool also drives the engine accessory gearbox.

HP turbine

The HP turbine is a single stage of nozzles and turbine blades which drive the compressor in exactly the same way as the LP turbine.

Free power turbine and reduction gearbox

Converting what would ordinarily be purely rearwards thrust into mechanical drive is made possible by the single-stage free power turbine. Installed immediately aft of the gas generator's turbine but operating independently (i.e. it is not connected mechanically to the moving parts of the engine), the FPT's disc is driven by the kinetic energy of the hot gases from the gas generator impinging on its blades. A hollow shaft running through the centre of the LP spool assembly connects to the aircraft's single-stage epicyclic reduction gearbox fitted in the air intake casing, in turn providing mechanical drive at the right speed to the main rotor gearbox.

A small take-off drives the FPT governor and FPT speed tachometer.

In the event of an engine failure, this mechanical independence from the main rotor gearbox also ensures that the transmission system is not compromised – a function previously played by the heavy clutch and freewheel assembly and associated cooling fan in the earlier piston-engined helicopters.

Engine oil system

Each engine is equipped with its own oil tank mounted at the front. The Mk.204 variant has an oil capacity of 8 pints (4.55 litres) while the Mk.205 has slightly more at 8½ pints (4.8 litres).

Engine fires

It goes without saying that having one – or both – of the engines catch fire in flight is a serious problem. With the engines contained within closed compartments at the rear of the aircraft, visible signs of engine fire could well take some time to become obvious to the crew without any automatic indication system in place.

To reduce the risk of fire in one engine spreading to either the other engine, the gearbox or the fuel tanks and avionic bay below, the engine bays are segregated by titanium firewalls – one between the two engines and one in front. The fuselage decking in this area is skinned not with aluminium (as per the rest of the airframe) but with titanium held in place with steel rivets that have greater high temperature-resisting properties.

While all of this helps to contain any fire, detecting it in the first place is vital. In order to do this, a 'firewire' system is used. Two of these firewire elements are installed, one in each engine bay, and consist of a thin stainless steel outer tube through which an electrode runs.

HOW THE ROLLS-ROYCE GEM WORKS

1. As the 'Start' button is pressed, the starter/generator is engaged which, via a driveshaft, turns the HP spool.
2. As the HP spool turns, so the HP compressor at the front draws air in and begins to compress it.
3. The compressed air is channelled via converging ducts into the annular reverse-flow combustion chamber. Here, fuel is sprayed in through four injector nozzles adjacent to the starter igniter plugs and the mixture ignited by a series of sparks generated by the high-energy igniter unit (HEIU).
4. As the mixture burns it rapidly expands and produces energy. This impinges on the HP turbine blades, causing the disc to turn and driving the HP compressor. As the hot gases travel further aft, they also flow over the LP turbine stage, making it rotate and in turn driving the LP compressor at the front of the engine to draw more air in.
5. The remaining hot gases then pass through the single-stage free power turbine making it rotate and, via a high torque shaft running forward through the two spool shafts, driving the engine reduction gearbox.
6. As the engine becomes self-sustaining, the starter/generator disengages and the HEIU stops. Fuel is now sprayed through 17 vaporising nozzles supplied by a fuel manifold assembly.

The electrode is insulated from the outer tube by a special filler.

If conditions within the engine bay exceed the normal operating temperature, the electrical impedance within the firewire sensing element increases. This change activates the relevant 'Fire Warning' indicator – depending upon which engine bay the fire has been detected in – situated on the fire control panel on the cockpit overhead console. Simultaneously, the red button fitted to the end of the associated engine conditioning lever will illuminate, together with the red 'FIRE' caption on the CWP and the crew will hear an audio warning through their helmets.

Fire extinguisher system

Each engine has its own dedicated fire extinguisher bottle and non-return valve situated in the upper rear avionic bay and delivery system, consisting of two fire suppression pipes, three delivery pipes and a three-way adapter installed in the engine bays themselves.

The No. 1 bottle, on the left-hand side, and No. 2 bottle on the right-hand side are filled with Freon 12B1 (otherwise known by the acronym BCF) extinguishant pressurised by nitrogen.

Having confirmed which engine is on fire, the Pilot or Observer will press the relevant numbered black and yellow striped button on the fire control panel. This sends a 28-volt DC electrical current to fire one of two cartridges fitted to the fire bottle. Extinguishant, under nitrogen pressure, is allowed to escape through the delivery pipes to the two fire suppression pipes – the outer pipes located along the outer lower edge of the engine bay and the inner pipes running up and along the top edge of the centre firewall – filling the compartment with Freon and hopefully suffocating the fire.

If, for whatever reason, this first attempt fails to put the fire out, all is not lost. A set of cross-feed pipes connecting the Number 1 and Number 2 systems together allows the unused contents of one bottle to be fed across to the opposite side. By setting the fire extinguisher 'CROSSFEED/NORMAL' switch to 'CROSSFEED' and depressing the same button again, the cartridge fitted on the cross-feed pipes of the opposite bottle fires, sending its contents through the delivery pipe to the affected engine bay, hopefully with the desired result.

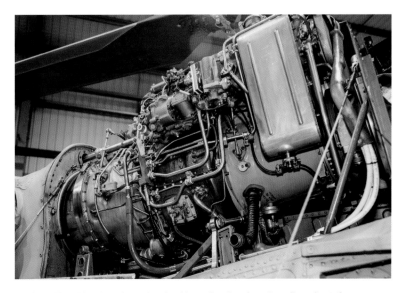

ABOVE The Number 2 engine looking aft, showing the oil tank at the forward end.

LEFT The red engine start buttons on the ends of the ECLs light up when an engine fire is detected to indicate which engine is affected. Simultaneously a red light in the centre of the associated fire extinguisher button (shown with yellow and black stripes) also illuminates.

BELOW The brown-coloured Number 2 engine fire extinguisher bottle with red and green connectors just visible in the aft equipment bay.

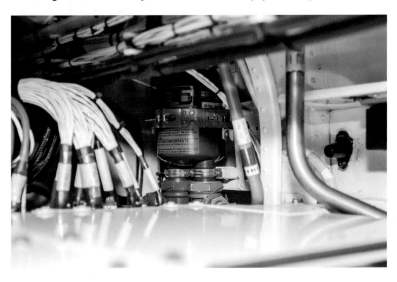

Chapter Four

Operating the Lynx

Aviation is undeniably demanding and dangerous, even in the best of conditions. But what about when your airfield is hardly bigger than the aircraft you are trying to land on it? And what about when that 'airfield' is rolling and pitching in a howling gale, in driving rain and hundreds of miles from land … and at night? It is then that those long hours of training begin to pay off. This is precisely what operating the Westland Lynx in a maritime role is all about.

OPPOSITE Conducting winch practice to the deck of Type 23 Frigate HMS *Sutherland*. As the helicopter's rotor blades spin through the air, they generate static electricity which will flow through the airframe and anything connected to it and must therefore be safely earthed to prevent an electric shock. Here, a member of the flight deck party is holding a 'zapper' rod to earth the Winchman before he comes into contact with the deck. The Winchman is often a trained junior member of the Flight, undertaking it as a secondary role. *(Simon Wilson)*

RIGHT Strike deep! No. 815 Naval Air Squadron's badge and motto displayed outside the squadron's new building at RNAS Yeovilton.

No. 815 Naval Air Squadron

In August 2014, 815 Naval Air Squadron (NAS) became the last Royal Navy unit to operate the Lynx, absorbing the training roles previously undertaken by 702 NAS. Thus began the swansong for the venerable Lynx, which was gradually being phased out of service and replaced by the new AgustaWestland Wildcat HMA Mk.2.

At its peak in the 1990s, 815 Naval Air Squadron consisted of approximately 500 personnel with a complement of Lynx HAS Mk.3 and Lynx HMA Mk.8 aircraft split between a Headquarters Flight and no fewer than 40 embarked Small Ships Flights. By the time of the withdrawal of the HAS Mk.3 variant, this had changed to three distinct elements: a Headquarters Flight with six aircraft; nine aircraft

of the embarked Flights; and three aircraft assigned to the Maritime Interdiction Flight. Its roles include the support of maritime counter-terrorism, supporting the Fleet Ready Escort (FRE), Response Force Task Group (RFTG) and contingency and provision and parenting of embarked Lynx Flights.

Headquarters Flight

The Headquarters Flight provides currency and refresher training for aircrew and engineers. Operational training, consisting of war fighting, anti-shipping/intelligence surveillance and reconnaissance (ISR), search and rescue, continental detachments and embarkation training is also provided.

Embarked Flights

Although the nine aircraft assigned to Royal Navy frigates and destroyers are 'parented' by 815 NAS they are all operated by individually numbered Flights. Each of these consists of ten personnel: a Pilot, an Observer, a Senior Maintenance Rating, three mechanical maintainer ratings, three avionic maintainer ratings and an Aircraft Controller.

Maritime Interdiction Flight

Three aircraft are provided for maritime counter-terrorism on 12 hours' standby, 365 days a year.

BELOW No. 815 NAS, 229 Flight, with their temporary Lynx HMA Mk.8, XZ729, on the flight deck of HMS *Monmouth*.

The aircrew

The Lynx, in its standard radar-configured role, is flown by a crew of two: the Pilot and the Observer.

Pilot

The Pilot is, as you would expect, the person who flies the aircraft. Ranked lieutenant or lieutenant commander, the Pilot could also be the Flight Commander, depending upon whether they are more senior than their Observer counterpart. They are in overall charge of the Flight and act as the aviation adviser to the ship's captain during embarked operations as well ensuring proper aviation practices are adhered to.

Observer

As with the Pilot, the Observer can be either of lieutenant or lieutenant commander rank. They can also be the Flight Commander if they are

LEFT No. 815 NAS 229 Flight's Flight Commander, Lieutenant Commander Simon 'Sharkey' Ward, RN, and Flight Observer, Lieutenant Keith Webb, RN, with their newly received Lynx HMA Mk.8, XZ725.

1. Helmet 4B/4L
2. White leather flying gloves
3. Life jacket
4. Short-term air supply system (STASS) bottle
5. Immersion suit
6. Survival aid pouch including first-aid kit and pyrotechnics
7. SARBE 7 and FastFind personal locator beacons
8. PSP connectors
9. Kneeboard with checklists
10. Aircraft check lists
11. Aircrew flying boots.

RIGHT Lieutenant Keith Webb, RN, gives Commander Philip Tilden, RN, Captain of HMS *Monmouth*, the night flying brief in the ship's operations room. The ship's Captain acts as flying authoriser when the Flight is embarked.

of a more senior rank than their right-hand-seat colleague. They do not, however, assume flying control of the aircraft; instead, their job is to 'fight' the aircraft in tactical situations, acting as the airborne combat systems officer, controlling the aircraft's sensors, mission systems, radar, radios and navigation equipment.

RIGHT No. 229 Flight Commander Lieutenant Commander Simon 'Sharkey' Ward, RN, continues the brief while LAC Sev Holbrook waits his turn in the background.

Winchman

Although the Observer often assumes the secondary role of Winchman – climbing out of their seat to the rear cabin to operate the winch when not required for navigational or tactical roles – it is preferable to have a dedicated individual to carry out this job. One of the Flight's maintainers, therefore, is also trained to act as a Winchman. It is a much-coveted secondary duty attracting, as it does, additional flying pay.

Briefing

Conducting a pre-flight briefing is an essential and mandatory part of operating any military aircraft safely. Normally an hour before the planned launch time, the crew of the aircraft convene in either the briefing room if ashore or the operations room if embarked in a ship. Here, the purpose of the sortie is discussed, together with all relevant information on the aircraft – which aircraft it is (only really relevant when ashore where more than one aircraft may be on the squadron's dispersal), its fuel load, range, launch time, sortie duration, destination, weapon fit, AUM, cargo and/or the number of passengers, any acceptable maintenance defects that the aircraft may be carrying – are all noted. A detailed brief is then given on the weather that might affect the aircraft along its planned sortie route, radio frequencies noted down for various air traffic control zones, any active danger areas and notices to airmen (NOTAMs) that might pose a danger en route. An authorising officer is present at the brief – the ship's captain if embarked – and they will need to be satisfied by those giving the brief that all of the planning is in order and that the aircrew are suitably qualified and 'current' (i.e. they have conducted sufficient recent training to undertake the sortie).

Walk-round checks

Having made sure that the paperwork is in order and signed to accept the aircraft, the crew now need to conduct physical checks of the Lynx to confirm that all is well. These inspections begin during the walk out to the aircraft with a quick overall look from a short distance for any obvious signs of damage or anything else that may appear untoward before beginning the detailed walk-round.

The first thing to check is the aircraft's Essential Safety Services Break (ESSB) switch and Master Armament Safety Switch (MASS) in the cockpit to make sure that they are selected to 'OFF' and 'GREEN' (safe) respectively, and that the fuel jettison switch on the overhead console is set to 'SHUT'. This is to ensure that if ground power is applied by the maintainers while conducting the walk-round that nothing unfortunate or embarrassing will happen.

Starting at the front of the nose, the walk-round is conducted in a clockwise direction along the starboard side and returning down the port side to ensure that everything is checked in a well-practised sequence.

First, the PID's red protective cover is removed and handed to the waiting groundcrew for safe storage. Opening the starboard gullwing door, the PID compressor pressure is checked before securing the door once again.

Looking up at the main gearbox sliding fairing, the Number 2 hydraulic system reservoir fluid level and Numbers 1 and 2 hydraulic system accumulator pressure gauges can be seen through Perspex windows built into the front of the fairing. The gauges should read between 60 and 70bar.

Next, the cabin door is slid forwards to allow the small footsteps built into the side of the

fuselage to be opened. Climbing up the side, the starboard main rotor gearbox footstep fairing can be unlatched and dropped down. Standing on the step built into the fairing, the main rotor head and area around it can be checked: the rubber boots around the spider pitch control arms, the collar around the mast, the lag plane dampers and the main rotor blade attachment pins.

Turning to the rear, the engine bay door locking T-bar is examined to make sure it is fully engaged and the pip pin holding it in place is secure.

Climbing back down on to the footsteps on the side of the aircraft, the main gearbox oil level sight is quickly noted (the sight glass on the port side will be checked later) before the footstep fairing is hinged back upwards and latched shut. Finally, the footsteps are pushed up into their locked positions flush with the fuselage.

Walking around the starboard undercarriage sponson, the green canvas flotation bag cover

ABOVE Standing on one of the footsteps in the side of the fuselage, the main rotor gearbox oil level sight glass is checked by opening the drop-down panel.

ABOVE The gust lock is removed from the tail rotor. Being so close to the stern, having someone to hold on to you is a good idea!

Below the engine door, the gravity and pressure refuel point caps (the latter under a spring-loaded flap) are checked for security and the static vent plug removed before seeing that the vent itself is clear of any obstruction. The same will be done on the port side.

The ESM aerials on the sponsons and the HF aerial with its wire antennae running down the starboard side of the tailcone are also inspected for security before arriving at the tail pylon hinge. Here the fixed hinge bolts are checked to make sure they are secure.

The final item to visually examine from the starboard side is the tailplane fitted at the top of the tail pylon before working around the rear of the tail, looking up at the white navigation light and anti-collision beacon for any signs of damage.

Now for the port side checks.

The first item is the tail rotor, checking the blades for scratches and dents and ensuring that the red-painted gust lock has been removed. Looking up, the oil levels for the tail rotor gearbox can be checked on the sight glass visible through a hole cut into the leading edge of the gearbox cowling. The oil level for the intermediate gearbox can also be checked by opening the small panel built into the side of the gearbox fairing.

Next is the tail pylon fold mechanism. Here, a quick check is performed to make sure that the locking pins are fully engaged and that the red warning flag is retracted flush with the tailcone and the ratchet lever is properly stowed.

Moving further forward, ensure the detachable panels built into the side of the tailcone for access to the tail rotor control cables and the quick-release fasteners holding the tail rotor drive shaft fairings are all secure.

Just aft of the port undercarriage sponson, the ground power supply connector should already have been plugged into the socket on the rear fuselage by the groundcrew or flight deck party. If the aircraft is embarked, the telebrief cable should also have been plugged in beneath the rear fuselage and safely anchored to the flight deck with a lanyard assembly.

Looking beneath the aircraft, the rubber fuel jettison pipe, Doppler aerials and deck lock harpoon should be checked for signs of damage and hydraulic leaks. Unlike more modern

is checked to make sure it is properly secured, there is the required 2in extension of oleo showing, that the blue-coloured wheel lock hydraulic lines are undamaged and that the wheel lock levers are set to 'ON'. The wheel tyres should be inspected for any obvious signs of cuts, wear and that the white creep marks painted across the tyre beading to the wheel rim are aligned. The wheels should already have been toed out by the groundcrew after the aircraft has been brought out on to the flight line (or flight deck) and be locked in position.

Standing back slightly to get a better view, the main gearbox oil cooler intake scoop, aft equipment bay fan intake and engine bay fire access points are all checked and the red engine exhaust blanks removed.

engines, the Gem is very much a product of its age and has a reputation for being somewhat oily; it is therefore not uncommon to find a small trace of oil running out of the engine bay drain port beneath the engine cowlings on both sides. This is quite normal.

Peering in through a small Perspex window on the side of the port undercarriage sponson, the pressure gauge for the Number 3 hydraulic system is checked.

Just like on the starboard side, the static plug is removed, the flotation bag cover is examined and the undercarriage checked before closing the port cabin door and the footsteps opened. Climbing up to open the drop-down footstep fairing, the port side areas of the main rotor head are checked and the main gearbox oil level is viewed through the sight glass before closing the fairing and climbing back down.

After ensuring the drop-down panels running along under the cabin floor are closed and the port gullwing doors are secure, the walk-round checks are complete.

Cockpit checks

The means by which the Pilot and Observer ensure that everything is in the right place before any engine or rotor start or before launch or recovery is the challenge and response technique. Taking the lead on this is the Observer, who will run through the Flight Reference Cards (FRCs). These flip cards contain brief lists of checks that are read aloud involving switch and

ALERT STATUSES

Alert State	Aircrew	Aircraft	Ship
5	Briefed, dressed, in aircraft	On spot, power on, switches made, circuit breakers in	Fly Stns
15	Briefed, dressed	On spot	Fly Stns
30	Briefed, dressed	Normally in hangar	Fly Stns
45	Stood down	Normally in hangar	Std down
45+		Undergoing maintenance	Std down

button positions and gauge readouts that are necessary to ensure safe operation. Having been 'challenged' by the Observer, the Pilot will carry out the check and give a verbal response which the Observer will then check against the FRCs to ensure that it is correct.

The Observer will busy himself by programming the aircraft's tactical system by punching in data via the CDNU on the interseat console.

Small-ship operations

It is mid-January 2016. HMS *Monmouth*, a Type 23 frigate, is exercising in Falmouth Bay south-west of the ship's home port of Plymouth. Capable of operating a Merlin helicopter, the ship has only recently returned to the fleet after refit and she is now conducting a period of work-up in readiness for her next deployment.

Firmly lashed to the flight deck at the ship's stern is Lynx HMA Mk.8 XZ729, which joined

BELOW The Type 23 Frigate HMS *Monmouth* in Falmouth Bay North.

LEFT With HMS *Monmouth* being affectionately known as 'The Black Duke', 229 Flight's own aircraft, XZ725, received unique black callsigns and deck letters as well as bespoke nose art.

the ship earlier from its 815 NAS base at RNAS Yeovilton. Still wearing the side number '452', deck letters 'DT' and titles HMS *Dauntless* from her previous ship, the aircraft has recently joined 229 Flight on a temporary basis while they await the delivery of their own aircraft.

Sadly, this is to be XZ729's swansong. A veteran of the Falklands, she had been severely damaged when a bomb dropped by an attacking

XZ729 – THE FALKLANDS SURVIVOR

LEFT Having carried out an attack on the Argentinian submarine *Santa Fe* off Grytviken, South Georgia, on 15 April 1982, Lynx HAS.2, XZ729 of 815 NAS, 221 Flight, HMS *Broadsword*, was badly damaged when a bomb burst through the ship's hangar during an attack by Skyhawk aircraft on 25 May. She is seen here at RNAY Fleetlands on 3 August having been delivered for repairs. *(RNAY Fleetlands)*

BELOW LEFT With the aircraft in the main airframe jig and the damaged cockpit section removed, a brand new assembly is prepared for fitting. *(RNAY Fleetlands)*

BELOW XZ729 still suspended in the jig with repairs almost complete. *(RNAY Fleetlands)*

Argentinian aircraft had ricocheted off the sea and through the side of HMS *Broadsword*'s hangar where the aircraft was stowed. The bomb smashed her nose off ahead of the windscreen before disappearing through the other side of the ship and falling into the sea – miraculously without exploding. Although severely damaged, XZ729 was brought back to the UK and extensively rebuilt at RNAY Fleetlands to live another day. After leaving HMS *Monmouth* to return to RNAS Yeovilton, her days are numbered as she is due to leave Somerset to be stripped for spares as part of the Wildcat Donor and Strip for Spares Programme where so many of her fellow stablemates have already gone.

'Hands to flying stations! Hands to flying stations!'

Broadcast over the ship's tannoy system, this rousing 'pipe', to use the proper naval term, is the order given, normally around 15 minutes in advance, for those personnel directly concerned to get to their respective stations to prepare for flying operations.

There are three key areas of control on board during flying operations: the bridge, where the Officer of the Watch will ensure that the ship is on a course that is not only suitable for the aircraft but safe for the ship, that certain transmitting systems are in the correct configuration and maintains control of the 'STOP/GO' lights on

RIGHT New cockpit, nose and roof installed and removed from the jig. *(RNAY Fleetlands)*

BELOW Fully repaired, refinished and ready for flight testing, XZ729 outside K Shop at RNAY Fleetlands in June 1984. *(RNAY Fleetlands)*

LEFT The flight deck markings on HMS *Monmouth* showing the deck lock grid, the landing spot, PEL ('bum') line, NVG cueing lines and vertical alignment lines on the hangar shutters.

CENTRE The horizon bars at the top of the hangar structure – fixed outer sections and a gyro-stabilised centre bar – which allow the Pilot to be aware of the horizon while concentrating on landing on the ship.

the flight deck; the operations room, where the leading aircraft controller will act as the on-board air traffic control officer and as the liaison between the aircraft and the ship; and the flight deck, where the FDO will conduct and manage the safe marshalling of the aircraft.

Flight deck markings

Operating a helicopter from the pitching, rolling flight deck of a small ship is arguably the most demanding aspect of naval aviation. Measuring just 45ft in width and 65ft in length – roughly the size of a tennis court – the flight deck is painted with a grey non-slip coating and has lashing hard points built in, NVD-compatible lighting and a series of lines painted to aid the Pilot in positioning the aircraft during recovery.

The middle of the landing area is identified by a white circle, in the centre of which is the deck lock grid. This rectangular, perforated plate is where the aircraft's deck lock harpoon engages to lock the helicopter to the flight deck. Running along the forward edge of the circle and extending to the left and to the right is a white line. Properly termed the Pilot's eye line (PEL), it is more commonly referred to as the 'bum line' as it should align with the Pilot's seat if the aircraft is landed in the right position, thus ensuring that the harpoon is located directly over the grid.

45-degree NVD cueing lines ahead of the PEL line aid with landing techniques at night, while a fore/aft line along the deck and vertical Pilot

LEFT At night, special NVD-compatible lighting bars outline the periphery of the hangar and flight deck. During helicopter operations, the hangar lighting is turned off and replaced with dim red lighting to protect the aircrew's night vision.

ABOVE With the tail of the aircraft being very close to the ship's stern when ranged, it is often spread while still in the hangar.

RIGHT The aircraft is moved out using the Douglas Ram Handler while maintainers walk alongside with wheel chocks at the ready in case control of the aircraft is lost.

alignment lines running up the hangar door screen also assist the Pilot in positioning the aircraft.

Around the periphery of the hangar structure and the flight deck edge are NVD-compatible LED lighting bars, while at the top of the hangar is the gyro-stabilised green LED-lit horizon bar.

Ranging the aircraft

As with all aircraft movements on board, permission to move the aircraft out of the hangar has to be obtained from the bridge, ensuring that the ship is on a steady course and not about to begin manoeuvring.

With the tail of the aircraft normally in very close proximity to the stern of the ship, it is generally safer to spread and lock it in place before leaving the hangar than trying to do so on the flight deck itself.

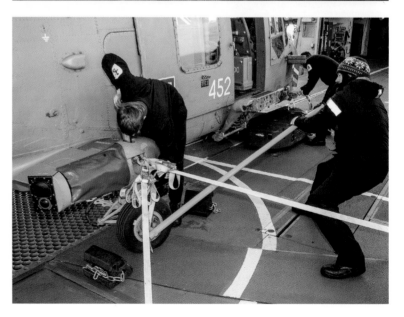

RIGHT Having been lashed to the deck, the mainwheels are toed out using a long bar pushed through the wheel hub before being locked in position.

1 The colour-coded stays (red for port) holding the main rotor head are removed …

2 … before the first blade is hinged forward into position using blade fold poles.

3 AET 'Meds' Meadows inserts the main rotor blade pin into position …

4 … before securing it in place with the 'spectacle' lock.

LEFT Before the start of flying operations, the flight deck party must carry out a 'FOD plod', scouring the deck area for any debris that may be sucked into the aircraft's engines and cause damage.

The aircraft is moved slowly out of the hangar using the Douglas Ram Handler with maintainers walking alongside with wheel chocks just in case anything goes wrong and the aircraft needs to be stopped quickly.

Engine start

With the aircraft ranged on the flight deck, it is secured using four nylon lashings (eight if the pitch and roll of the ship exceeds certain limits and/or the harpoon is not engaged in the deck lock grid), the four main rotor blades and the tail pylon spread and locked in position and the tanks refuelled according to the sortie type and expected duration.

The maintainers have conducted their before-flight (BF) inspections ahead of handing the aircraft over to the Pilot who, along with the Observer, have both carried out their own external walk-round checks and internal pre-start checks. Having now strapped into their seats they are at 'Alert 5'.

The Pilot signals to the FDO for permission to start the Number 1 engine. At night this is done by switching the port and starboard coloured navigation lights to shine steady bright. The FDO calls the ship's bridge over his intercom to ask the Officer of the Watch if the ship has turned on to a steady course in preparation for launching the helicopter. The Officer of the Watch has the responsibility to conduct mandatory launch and recovery checks, ensuring that the approach and departure lanes are clear, that the ship is on a steady course with no immediate intention to begin manoeuvring and at the right speed, the relative wind, pitch and roll are in limits and that any communication and radar systems are in a safe configuration.

After the bridge has radioed back to confirm the ship's course, the FDO quickly checks his anemometer and wind direction gauges and compares the figures with his ship helicopter operating limit (SHOL) charts to ensure that the conditions are right to continue. Turning back to face the aircraft he then signals to the Pilot to start Number 1 engine. With the engine started, the maintainer who has been standing guard with a fire extinguisher will move to the other side of the aircraft whereupon the Pilot will signal back to the FDO for permission to start Number 2 engine.

STARTING THE LYNX

1. The Pilot will check that the ACC DRIVE/MAIN DRIVE on the overhead panel is set to 'ACC DRIVE'. A corresponding amber caution will appear on the CWP. Rotor brake should be set to 'ON'.

2. Number 1 engine is started and the engine conditioning lever (ECL) advanced to 95% engine speed (Ng). Still in 'ACC DRIVE', the power from the engine drives only the accessories gearbox. As it does so, both of the alternators come on line at 78% and all three of the hydraulic systems will indicate 140bar pressure. The MRGB oil pressure gauge will also begin to start indicating.

3. Number 2 engine is now started. With the rotor brake applied, however, the engine's FPT will not turn and power will not be transmitted into the MRGB.

4. Before the Number 2 engine reaches 65%, the rotor brake is released. The Number 2 engine FPT begins to turn, causing the MRGB gearing to turn. As it does so, the main and tail rotors begin to rotate.

5. The Number 2 engine ECL is now advanced to the flight idle gate. As the FPT increases in speed, so the starboard through shaft takes over the running of the accessories gearbox due to the different number of teeth on the gearing described earlier.

6. No longer driving the accessories gearbox, the Number 1 engine ECL is now retarded to the ground idle gate. This activates safety interlock microswitches to allow power to the acc drive actuator.

7. After checking that the two engines are indeed operating at different speeds with Number 1 engine running slower than the Number 2, the Pilot will select the overhead switch to 'MAIN DRIVE'.

8. The acc drive actuator will motor the outer bearing housing along the port through shaft to engage with the set of cams. As the two mesh together, the shaft begins to turn, providing power through to the MRGB main conformal gear. A mechanical 'doll's-eye' indicator on the overhead console will confirm this.

9. With both engines now successfully coupled to and running the MRGB, the Number 1 engine ECL can be slowly advanced to the flight idle gate to match the Number 2 engine.

10. With the Number 2 engine effectively running the accessories gearbox it is important to check that, in the event of the engine failing, the Number 1 engine will be able to take over. To do this, the Number 2 engine ECL is slightly retarded. As the speed of the starboard through shaft decreases, so the port shaft driven by the Number 1 engine should take over automatically. This freewheel speed (Nf) split is shown on the cockpit triple tachometer gauge.

11. The Number 2 engine ECL is now reset to 'FLIGHT IDLE' and the speed select lever (SSL) advanced to 107% to increase the rotor speed (Nr) ready for launch.

Engaging rotors

Now ready to engage the rotors, the Pilot will signal his request to the FDO. At night the navigation lights are switched from steady bright to flashing dim. The FDO calls to the Officer of the Watch on the bridge once again.

'Bridge, flight deck: permission to engage rotors on "452".'

As with the engine starts, this is to ensure that the ship has not altered course or is about to do so. Any sudden manoeuvring by the ship at this stage could cause damage to the main rotor head.

'Flight deck, bridge: engage rotors on "452".'

With permission from the bridge granted, the FDO signals to the Pilot to engage rotors by briefly whirling one finger (or illuminated wand if at night) above his head.

ENGAGING ROTORS

1. Retard Number 1 Engine ECL to 'GROUND IDLE'
2. Engage rotor
3. Put Number 1 engine into 'MAIN DRIVE'
4. Advance Number 1 Engine ECL to 'MAX'.

BELOW The FDO, Petty Officer Tim Rowe, checks his anemometer and wind direction gauges.

Launch

As the aircrew bring the aircraft's systems online a constant flow of information is passed over the secure telebrief cable from the leading aircraft controller, including ship's course and speed, pressure settings for barometric instruments, aircraft configuration details, weights and endurance figures. With the cockpit checks almost complete, the Pilot gives the FDO a 2-minute warning. The FDO relays this to the flight deck crew by holding up two fingers or both lit wands. One of the flight deck party will be cleared by the FDO to enter the rotor disc area and check along the sides of the aircraft to make sure that all panels and doors are secured. Once the Pilot is ready to launch, the port and starboard navigation lights will be switched from steady to flashing. This is the cue for the FDO and the flight deck captain, who are standing on the opposite side of the flight deck, to look forward along either side of the ship. This 'checking the air lanes' is to make sure that there is nothing ahead of the ship which might pose a danger to the aircraft as it lifts off the flight deck.

'Bridge, flight deck: ready to launch "452".'

'Flight deck, bridge: launch "452".'

As the Officer of the Watch on the bridge switches the 'STOP/GO' light positioned to the left of the hangar door to green, the FDO quickly checks his instruments and SHOL charts one last time. The four flight deck party members – known at this stage as the 'lashing numbers' – are given permission to walk out to the aircraft and after receiving the 'away lashings' signal from the FDO, start to remove the nylon straps holding the aircraft to the deck. With these gone, the aircraft is now held in place purely by negative pitch applied to the main rotor blades and the harpoon engaged in the flight deck grid. Waiting for permission from the FDO to leave the rotor disc area, the four lashing numbers walk back to the hangar door. As they get there, they turn to face the aircraft and hold each of their lashings above their heads to show the Pilot that all of them have been removed. At night, the FDO will shine one of his lit wands on each of the lashings as they are held aloft to allow the Pilot to see them clearly.

The FDO now gives the 'Out deck lock' signal to the Pilot to disengage the harpoon.

LEFT With the nylon lashings removed, the FDO gives the lashing numbers permission to leave the aircraft's rotor disc …

With the Pilot ensuring minimum pitch on ground (MPOG) is applied to the collective lever, creating negative pitch on the main rotor blades and a force of up to 3,000lb (1,360kg) to pin the aircraft down on to the deck, the deck lock harpoon is retracted. As the harpoon withdraws, the captain of the flight deck turns his thumbs-down signal (or downward-pointing red wand at night) to a thumbs-up as a visual confirmation to the Pilot who will already have felt a jolt through the airframe.

With a quick glance to the right to make sure that the green light from the bridge is still showing, the FDO faces the aircraft with both

BELOW … who then hold up the lashings clearly to confirm to the Pilot that they have all been removed.

RIGHT With the Pilot judging the right moment to launch, the aircraft lifts swiftly off the deck. Note the angle of the horizon.

BELOW As the aircraft lifts, the telebrief cable anchored to the deck is pulled out, severing the secure communications link to the ship ...

arms held out level before swiftly raising them until they are vertical, signalling the Pilot to 'come up'.

The exact moment at which the aircraft leaves the deck is at the discretion of the Pilot who will wait until the movement of the ship is within limits for a launch. If the weather is rough, being connected to a pitching, rolling flight deck can be an uncomfortable experience, so getting airborne promptly is generally a good idea.

As the Pilot pulls up on his collective lever, the aircraft swiftly lifts off the deck and into a 10–15ft hover until the stabilised horizon bar at the top of the hangar is at eye level. As it does so, the telebrief cable anchored to the deck is pulled out, severing the telebrief communication link between the aircraft and the ship.

Holding this steady position momentarily while the Pilot and Observer complete their after take-off checks, the FDO then directs the Pilot to move the aircraft left by holding his right arm horizontally and bending and unbending his left arm at the elbow with his hand touching his head. It is important to minimise the time spent hovering above the deck as there is every chance that in bad weather the pitching deck

could suddenly come up and strike the aircraft.

As the aircraft slides left away from the deck the FDO gives one final 'clear' signal and the Pilot transitions from the hover into forward flight along the port side of the aircraft, accelerating to 80 knots into the port air lane and away.

'Flight deck, all positions: aircraft "452" launched to port.'

With this call, the Leading Aircraft Controller (LAC) deep within the ship's operations room assumes control of the aircraft from the FDO.

Landing

To begin a recovery to the ship, the aircraft will join the circuit downwind – flying parallel with but in the opposite direction – at 400ft and normally along the port side of the ship which has turned on to a flying course. Using the standard 'clock code', when the aircraft reaches a point at which the ship is in its 8 o'clock position a gentle 20-degree banked turn to port will be initiated, reducing speed to 60 knots to be positioned on the correct glide path angle known as the ship's 'Red 165'; this brings the aircraft into a position parallel with the flight deck but clear of the ship's

ABOVE ... before transitioning into forward flight along the flight lane down the port side of the ship.

1 The FDO gives the signal 'ready to receive' to the Lynx as it calls 'final' on approach to the ship along its bearing 'Red 165'.

superstructure so that it can fly away safely in the event of any emergency.

At ½nm distant the aircraft will call 'Final' to the LAC in the operation room. During the final approach the Observer will go through the pre-landing checks listed in the FRCs with the Pilot responding accordingly. The undercarriage wheel locks are set to 'IN' and the deck lock harpoon set to 'ON' ready for use. On the flight deck the FDO will assume the 'ready to receive' position with both arms held up in a Y shape. As the aircraft comes in alongside the flight deck and stabilises in a 10ft hover, the FDO signals the Pilot to start to move to starboard across the deck.

At night, the gyro-stabilised horizon bar at the top of the ship's hangar will be switched on when the aircraft is 1½ miles out. The Observer

2 The aircraft is marshalled forward ...

3 AND 4 ... given the signal to hold steady in a hover momentarily alongside ...

5 AND 6 ... before sliding right across the deck ...

7 AND 8 ... and given the signal to 'come down'.

will switch the external navigation lights from steady to flashing bright and switch off the anti-collision beacon.

The aim is to land the aircraft such that the deck lock harpoon is centred over the deck lock grid. As the aircraft transitions across the grid the FDO will give the 'come down' signal at which point the Pilot will swiftly lower the collective lever. After the wheels touch the flight deck the Pilot will engage the harpoon to extend after pushing the collective lever fully down and through to the MPOG setting to ensure the aircraft is firmly on the deck and to minimise the risk of it sliding around if the ship's motion is excessive.

With the harpoon engaged, the FDO will direct the flight deck party to move quickly in under the helicopter's rotor disc and start applying the nylon lashings between the deck and the tie-down rings on the nose and the undercarriage sponsons. Once they are securely in place and tightened, the FDO will direct the flight deck party away from the aircraft, having first obtained permission from the Pilot.

The Pilot will now carry out the 'stopping the rotors with engine running' checks, ensuring that all switches are in the right positions. First, the Number 2 engine will be retarded, followed by the Number 1, which is left in accessory drive condition. As the engines wind down, the flying controls are operated to exhaust the hydraulic system of pressure and the right-hand

9 As the wheels hit the deck, the deck lock harpoon is selected …

10 … it successfully engages with the grid with the jaws snapping shut …

11 … and the harpoon begins to retract under hydraulic pressure, drawing the aircraft down on to the deck and compressing the nose oleo.

BELOW With the aircraft safely shut down, the Pilot and Observer exit the cockpit while additional lashings are attached.

yaw pedal is pushed fully forward to unload the spring bias unit and leave it in a safe condition.

The rotor speed is allowed to decay naturally until it reaches the maximum speed at which the rotor brake can be safely applied. The Pilot now applies the brake, carefully gauging the amount by which the rotor slows to ensure that the main rotor blades stop at a 45-degree position. This is important as it keeps the rearmost blades safely away from the still-hot engine exhausts, heat from which could easily damage the composite structure of the blades.

Finally, all the aircraft's electrical systems are switched off. The crew will climb out and, after a walk-round of the aircraft to look for any damage that might have occurred during flight, make their way back to the SMR's office at the top of the aircraft hangar for a debrief of the aircraft's serviceability state and report on any faults found to allow maintenance activities to be planned. The MF700 will be filled out with the relevant sortie details and the aircraft signed back in. The Lynx is now firmly back in the hands of the engineers who will already be

LEFT The Flight Commander, Lieutenant Commander Ward, gives a verbal debrief of any issues found with the aircraft to the SMR, CPO 'Cakey' Eccles.

BELOW If the aircraft is remaining on deck then the various blanks and covers must be attached to give protection. Putting on the main rotor blade 'tip socks', which allow the blades to be tied down, can be tricky on a pitching, rolling deck, requiring the step ladder to be securely lashed down as well.

ABOVE The Lynx being prepared for launch. The blue light in the cabin is from one of the maintainer's head torches, the light being less damaging to the crew's night vision.

LEFT The FDO's wands blurred by the long exposure as he gives permission for the lashing numbers to enter the aircraft's rotor disc.

BELOW A long-exposure shot of a landing at night, showing the light trails left by the port (red) and starboard (green) navigation lights as the aircraft slides right across the deck and lands. The FDO and his wands have become something of a frenzied blur!

busy refuelling it, fitting tip socks to the main rotor blades to prevent them from flapping in the wind, installing engine intake and exhaust blanks and pitot and static covers and plugs to protect the various systems.

Stowing the aircraft

Although the Lynx can remain safely lashed to the flight deck, it is preferable to afford it better protection from the heavily salt-laden atmosphere by bringing it back into the hangar. It is not unknown for sudden freak waves – so-called 'goffers' – to break over the stern of the ship, ripping out the nylon lashings, causing the deck lock harpoon to fail and the aircraft to be washed overboard.

Despite its size, the Lynx cannot fit into the ship's hangar in the fully spread configuration. Therefore, the tail pylon and main rotor blades must first be folded and secured. The red-painted gust lock is attached to the tail rotor to prevent it from being damaged by any sudden gusts of wind. The tail is then folded by operating the ratchet mechanism on the port side to disengage the locking pins holding the tail pylon to the tailcone. As the tail folds to the starboard side, a hold-back hook on the pylon engages with a latch mechanism on the tailcone to keep it securely in position.

Next, the main rotor blades are folded. A specially designed carrying pole with a shaped pocket arrangement on the end is used to hold each blade in turn – starting with the rearmost set – while a maintainer on the top of the aircraft retracts one of the two blade pins holding the blade in position. As the pin is removed, the blade is able to pivot around the remaining pin, allowing the maintainers with the pole to walk the blade backwards and secure it in a special cradle that has been fitted to the tailcone. The procedure is repeated for all four blades until they are all hinged to point rearwards and secured in their own blade-fold stowages. Finally, one end of a set of metal rods are installed on the forwardmost main rotor head blade extension arms and the other secured to spigots on the cabin roof to prevent the main rotor head from turning.

As with ranging the aircraft, the Lynx can normally be moved using a Douglas Ram Handler. The rechargeable battery-powered

LEFT A fully folded feline!

BELOW The Lynx is brought in using a combination of the Douglas Ram Handler and running lashings assisted by additional members of the ship's company when the sea state is sufficiently rough to risk the aircraft sliding on the deck.

system, also sometimes used ashore when a towing tractor is not available, is capable of moving the fully fuelled and armed aircraft by engaging with the nosewheel of the aircraft and lifting it off the ground. A suitably trained maintainer can then operate and control the handler using a remote control unit slung around their neck.

If the weather is poor and the motion of the ship too great, however, the aircraft will be brought in using what are termed 'running lashings'. Taking the front lashings and attaching them to the next set of forward hard points on the deck, they are then carefully tightened while at the same time loosening the rear nylon lashings to allow the aircraft to be inched forward on the deck. This repetitive process takes some time, but it ensures that the aircraft is safely controlled by being secured to the deck at all points in the process.

With the aircraft safely within the confines of the ship's hangar, it is secured to the deck with a minimum of five steel chains – three on each of the main oleos and one either side of the nose – and wheel chocks to ensure that it cannot move. Steel gags – painted bright red as all such ground locks are to make them more visible during walk-round checks – are also clamped around the exposed areas of the oleos to prevent the aircraft from bouncing up and down.

LEFT Steel chain lashings attached to the port undercarriage sponson and red-painted oleo gag to prevent movement in rough seas or during ship manoeuvring.

Chapter Five

Maintaining the Lynx

If flying the Lynx can perhaps be considered as the 'glamorous' part of operating the aircraft, then the unglamorous element is undoubtedly the engineering work needed to achieve that flying capability. With aircraft now nearly three decades old and based on an initial design concept from the 1960s, the men and women of 815 Naval Air Squadron have their work cut out to keep these old workhorses serviceable.

OPPOSITE Mobile tool kits are provided to allow maintenance to be carried out on the line. The badge on the nose incorporates the white horse of Kent, this being Lynx HMA Mk.8, ZD257, '425/KT', of 815 NAS, 217 Flight, HMS *Kent*.

NO SMOKING

Getting the aircraft to the ship is relatively easy. Looking after it while it is there is a much more difficult logistical exercise. A deployable spares pack (DSP) consisting of items that are deemed likely to be required during a lengthy deployment must be packed on board in the confines of the hangar, including items such as spare engines and (as seen here) spare main rotor blades.

As a unit which 'parents' ship's Flights, 815 NAS is effectively split between shore and embarked operations. Conducting and coordinating the maintenance of the aircraft, some of which can be on the other side of the world, can therefore be a particular challenge.

Geographical location of the aircraft brings with it another issue. Some tasks that may seem quite simple and straightforward while the aircraft is in benign conditions (safely on land) can often turn out to be the most difficult and dangerous to achieve when at sea. Take, for instance, changing a wheel: to get the wheel off, the aircraft will need jacking – easy enough in a stable, level hangar at Yeovilton – but when that hangar is on the back of a ship in the South Atlantic and constantly rolling and pitching up and down, the aircraft is liable to suddenly slip off the jack and become severely damaged and likely injure someone nearby in the process.

Ship's Flight

An embarked ship's Flight comprises ten individuals, including the Pilot and Observer, all working together as a close-knit team to maintain and operate the Lynx both ashore and at sea. Being away from base for months on end, the team has to be able to operate as an autonomous unit, capable of carrying out all tasks from basic maintenance through to repair and modification work wherever the aircraft or the ship may be.

Three Air Engineering Technicians (AETs) of the mechanical trade – titled M1, M2 and M3 – look after the mechanical aspects of the aircraft. In the Fleet Air Arm, these are often known by their nicknames of 'grubbers' due to their work often being dirty through the use of oils, greases and fluids.

Their opposite numbers, the AETs of the avionic trade, are known as 'greenies': a term originating from the green-coloured cloth once worn by electrical engineering officers to denote their trade. Three of these – titled AV1, AV2 and AV3 – look after all of the aircraft's electrical system, including the radar and radios. These two roles were once separate with the radar and radio work being undertaken by 'pinkies': a now-defunct term whose origins lay with the pink-coloured forms for radio and radar equipment held within the aircraft MF700 aircrew servicing form.

M1 and AV1 are the senior ratings at petty officer rank. Normally the M1 will also double as a flying maintainer. Given specific training in the simulator to enhance their knowledge of emergency procedures, ECL management and basic airmanship, the flying maintainer acts as a left-hand seat member of the crew. They can also conduct ground runs on the aircraft. They do not, however, receive any training on navigation, nor are they expected to use the aircraft's radios. The M2 and AV2 positions are normally leading hands while the M3 and AV3 roles are filled by leading air engineering technicians.

Coordinating this team is the senior supervisor – the Senior Maintenance Rating (SMR). A chief petty officer, the SMR is accountable for the airworthiness of the aircraft, overseeing and signing for all maintenance activities carried out as well as being the liaison between the maintenance and flying sides of the aircraft's operation.

Last, but by no means least, is the Leading Aircraft Controller (LAC). Although very much part of the Flight, this person does not conduct any maintenance on the aircraft. Instead they act as the Flight's personal air traffic controller when

ABOVE The Flight's maintainers and supervisors on the flight deck awaiting the aircraft's return from a sortie. All personnel on the flight deck during operations must wear protective headgear and goggles as well as life jackets.

BELOW All aircraft should be electrically earthed for safety while in the hangar.

ABOVE Getting access to the various parts of the aircraft requires specialist aluminium staging which can be positioned alongside the fuselage even with the main rotor blades still fitted.

RIGHT With the engines surrounded by titanium firewalls, access for maintenance is extremely tight. Accidentally dropping tools into inaccessible areas is a constant hazard.

embarked, their place of work being in the ship's operations room, where they monitor the radar and communicate with the aircraft via radio.

Carrying the responsibility for all of the squadron's Flights is the Air Engineering Officer (AEO). Normally of lieutenant commander rank, the AEO is directly accountable to the squadron CO and has the task, among a wide range of other things, of upholding engineering standards and practices.

Maintenance types

There are two main basic types of maintenance – scheduled and unscheduled. Scheduled maintenance includes such tasks as flight servicing (FS), which is carried out immediately before (BFS) and after (AFS) each flight and during turn-round (TR) between sorties.

It also includes larger work packages, which are planned at different hourly and monthly frequencies – 25-hourly, 50-hourly, 75-hourly, etc. – according to the aircraft's maintenance schedules. These can involve careful inspections of flight-critical components using anything from the naked eye through to more sophisticated non-destructive testing (NDT) techniques, as well as the more routine tasks such as the replenishment of oils and lubrication.

Some inspections are one-offs, carried out a certain number of hours after a component has been replaced, while others will be repetitive, especially if a particular fault has been found which requires constant monitoring to determine whether the problem has stabilised or is getting worse and further remedial action is required.

To assist with the maintenance planning and identification of the work, the maintenance schedule divides the aircraft into systems and subsystems as well as zones. System 40, for instance, covers the powerplant; 40-20 is the identifier for the engine controls. Part of this falls into Zone 164.

The biggest of the planned events were depth maintenance work packages (originally known as Scheduled Base Maintenance). From the late 1970s until 2015 these were carried out at Fleetlands – initially as the Royal Naval Aircraft Yard (RNAY), then Naval Aircraft Repair Organisation (NARO), Defence Aviation Repair Agency (DARA) and finally Vector Aerospace Helicopter Services (VAHS) – and saw the aircraft being extensively stripped to components, inspected, parts either repaired or replaced, systems modified and upgraded, the external surfaces refinished, rebuilt and flight tested. Each depth activity was carried out in accordance with a 600-hour rolling calendar.

Many of the aircraft's components are 'lifed' – the amount of time, measured in either calendar days or months or flying hours, that it is designed safely to be operated for. The timely replacement of these parts to ensure that the optimum amount of usage is gained from them – while not exceeding their lifing limit and not impacting on the availability of an aircraft by trying to conduct as many planned changes in one maintenance package – is a challenge.

Unscheduled maintenance is basically any work that has not been forecast. Faults reported by aircrew at the end of a sortie or by maintainers during scheduled maintenance fall into this category. This emergent work is impossible to predict. To minimise its impact on serviceability, it is important to have sufficient spares and trained manpower available and capable of dealing with any eventuality as it arises. To meet operational requirements in the most efficient way possible, the engineering team led by the AEO and the SMR will prioritise work accordingly.

The 'watch' system

To ensure that there are sufficient levels of manpower available to undertake the necessary maintenance on the squadron at any one time, the Fleet Air Arm operate what is termed the 'watch' system with each watch consisting of between six and twelve maintainers.

The first of these is the '24 about' 'port and starboard watch'. The port watch will arrive for work (or 'turn to' in naval parlance) at midday and work until 10.00pm, come back in at 7.00am the following day and work until midday; at this point the starboard watch will turn to and work the same hours, effectively giving the port watch 24 hours off. This routine works well and allows a level of continuity with

LEFT Repairs form part of maintenance activities. Here, a maintainer rivets a new aluminium skin on to the port engine door inner face.

ABOVE Tail rotor gust locks, dehumidifier adaptors and wheel chocks stowed in the corner of the hangar.

receive a handover from one watch, work until 7.00am and hand over to the next watch.

For embarked operations, however, there are not enough maintainers to sustain this particular routine and therefore a '12-about' watch is observed, nominally working between 7.00am and 7.00pm, 12 hours on and 12 hours off.

Corrosion

Capable of being deployed anywhere in the world, maritime aircraft often operate in some of the most hostile environments in aviation. Arguably the most damaging of these is salt water.

Corrosion is the deterioration of a material by chemical interaction with the surrounding environment. It is, without doubt, the most persistent and repetitive defect found in aircraft operating at sea. If left undetected and unchecked, it can have a significant impact on the longevity of components, the availability of the aircraft for tasking and, in the worst-case scenario, lead to catastrophic failures with the loss of the aircraft and, potentially, the crew.

Fluids such as salt water, oil, fuel and cleaning compounds can permeate through

ABOVE Tail rotor gust locks, dehumidifier adaptors and wheel chocks stowed in the corner of the hangar.

not too many watch handovers, reducing the risk of something being missed or forgotten.

So what about overnight? For this, a third type of watch is introduced: the 'slips watch'. These individuals come in at 10.00pm to

BELOW Operating aircraft at sea brings with it problems associated with salt water corrosion. Here, HAS Mk.3, XZ233, is treated to an early bath using foam detergent followed by a rinse with clean, fresh water to remove all salt deposits.

joints and seals in the aircraft's structure, can become trapped in inaccessible areas and remain there for long periods of time between depth maintenance cycles. The highly corrosive emulsion can quickly begin to eat away at any unprotected aluminium alloy structure and start to impact on its strength and integrity.

With the Lynx operating off the flight deck of a Type 23 frigate just 16ft above the sea, the downwash from the main rotor can cause recirculation of the water, coating the aircraft in a fine mist of highly corrosive salt water. Corrosion found around the cockpit frames and the transportation joint is therefore not an uncommon occurrence.

Husbandry

Keeping the deterioration of the aircraft and its components under control comes under the general heading of 'husbandry'.

The Lynx, as with all other aircraft, is subject to routine external fresh water and foam washes to remove any corrosive substances such as salt and engine exhaust compounds that may have accumulated on the airframe during the course of operations. Likewise, the

LEFT Maintenance of the surface finish is an important part of 'husbandry' as it protects the airframe from corrosion.

LEFT Leading Hand Rory Lowther sprays fresh water over the tail rotor of **XZ725** after arriving back at RNAS Yeovilton after being embarked in HMS *Monmouth*. This will remove any salt water deposits.

RIGHT AND FAR RIGHT After conducting winching at sea, the hoist can become contaminated with salt water which can lead to corrosion. Here, the cable is gradually pulled out during maintenance and run through a bucket of clean, fresh water.

BELOW With 100ft of cable, it takes a few maintainers and a lot of space in the hangar to pull the cable all the way out.

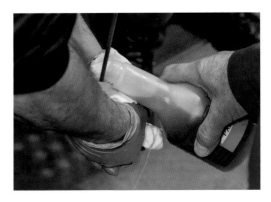

Gem engines are given compressor washes – 'comp washes' – using both clean water and industrial cleaning chemicals to rinse through the compressor blades. After conducting wet-winching, the winch cable is carefully unwound from the drum and rinsed through a bucket of fresh water before being coated in light water-repelling oil and wound back in.

Dehumidifying equipment is also used to pump fresh air through grilles and vents in the nose and aft equipment bays to help reduce the amount of moisture, which might otherwise interfere with sensitive electronics.

FAR LEFT AND LEFT Having washed the cable, it is slowly motored back on to the drum while pouring a water-repelling oil on to it to help keep corrosion at bay.

BELOW LEFT AND BELOW In order to keep various sensitive electronics in the nose and aft equipment bays completely dry while in the hangar, as seen here, or on board ship, special dehumidification units can be attached using adapters (seen here in red) to grilles and vents to pump fresh air through.

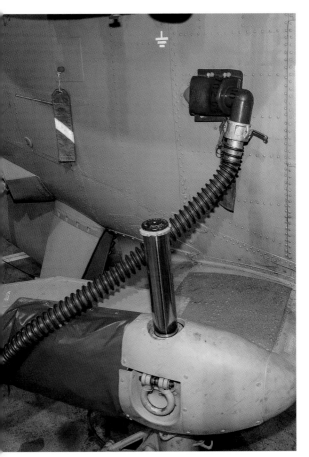

LEFT A three-digit callsign number is carried on both cabin doors. This number is unique to the Flight's parented ship – in this case HMS *Dauntless*. The Union Flag was originally applied to aircraft during the Armilla Patrol in the Persian Gulf and has been a feature of all subsequent embarked aircraft ever since. A RN corporate logo is also applied for good measure.

PAINT SCHEMES

The Lynx HMA Mk.8 is finished in the standard maritime camouflage of overall Medium Sea Grey (BS381C-637). On average, some 16 litres of paint is used to surface refinish a Lynx. Unit markings, such as parent ship deck letters, callsigns, Royal Navy corporate logos and Union Flags are applied in Spandex to specifically designated areas which are first prepared with a coating of gloss varnish. This allows the markings to be removed easily and without damage to the underlying paint.

The only exceptions to this standard scheme were one HAS Mk.3 (XZ250) and two HMA Mk.8 aircraft (XZ692 and XZ722) which had a special 'Black Cats' markings applied by the Serco paint shop at RNAS Yeovilton. Using an overhead projector, the markings were projected on to the side of the aircraft before being traced on to the fuselage using chalk. The resulting lines were then masked up and the markings painted in.

RIGHT Complementing the callsign number is the parent ship's deck letter ident, applied to the knife edge fairing at the rear of the tail pylon.

RIGHT National markings are a legally mandated requirement to allow the aircraft's identity and origin to be determined. Here, the roundel – applied to all British military aircraft – on the rear fuselage is painted in 'Pale Ident Blue' and 'Pale Ident Red' (not pink!).

RIGHT The parent ship's name is carried on the front of the radome.

BS381C-172	Pale Ident Blue	Roundels
BS381C-356	Golden Yellow	Emergency markings
BS381C-454	Pale Ident Red	Roundels
BS381C-538	Cherry Red	Danger markings
BS381C-637	Medium Sea Grey	Fuselage
BS381C-638	Dark Sea Grey	Interior
	White	National markings, stencils
	Black	Cabin protective floor panels

LEFT Having used an overhead projector to project the artwork on to the aircraft and the lines lightly marked on to the surface using chalk, paint shop supervisor Marcus Brakes carefully masks the intricate Black Cat design on to HMA Mk.8, XZ692, before applying the paint.

ABOVE XZ692 fully marked up ready for the paint to be applied.

RIGHT Pride of ownership is an important factor in building the teamwork so vital during often lengthy deployments. Many Flights have taken to the old tradition of naming their aircraft and bestowing associated artwork upon them. 'Miss Fit' is one such example of recent nose art.

ABOVE A full suite of technical publications must also be sent with the aircraft to allow maintenance to be carried out.

Vibration

All helicopters, no matter how big or small, naturally vibrate. If vibration is not kept within specific limits, it can quickly cause significant structural damage and in the worse cases lead to the loss of an aircraft. Certain areas of the Lynx have, of course, been reinforced over the years during the various upgrade programmes, most notably the transportation joint and area between the cockpit and the control frame, which have all had additional strengthening plates introduced in a bid to improve the stiffness.

When two mating surfaces rub together as a result of vibration, they are said to 'fret'. This fretting action can quickly cause the material to wear away and, if mixed with fluids, generate tell-tale abrasive compounds known as 'fretting juice'. Dirty circles of this substance can often be found around the heads or tails of 'working' rivets, which must be replaced.

Maintenance records

As with any aircraft, any maintenance carried out on the Lynx has to be formally recorded and signed for by suitably qualified and experienced personnel. In order to do this, maintainers must adhere to laid-down procedures contained within a suite of air publications (APs). These are the 'real' Haynes Manuals, covering all aspects of the aircraft's operation and maintenance. Broken down into numerically prefixed 'topics', the first six are primarily aimed at providing information relating to the maintenance of the aircraft:

Topic 1 *The Aircrew Maintenance Manual*, covering all general and technical information as well as installation and removal instructions for all components.

Topic 2 *Approved Modification Leaflets* applicable to the aircraft.

Topic 3 *The Illustrated Parts Catalogue*, giving a detailed breakdown of the aircraft and its assemblies and listing all spares needed to maintain the aircraft.

Topic 5 *Maintenance Schedules*, listing all of the calendar-based and hourly-based inspections that must be adhered to in order to keep the aircraft serviceable.

Topic 6 *The Aircraft Repair Manual*, detailing the limitations of structural damage allowable, the approved methods of repair and the tools and materials needed to carry them out.

OILS, FUELS AND LUBRICANTS

Standard fuels:	AVTUR (F34), AVTAG (F40), AVCAT (F44)	
Alternative fuels:	AVTUR (F35)	Not to be used at fuel temperatures below +5°C in flight
Emergency fuels:	AVGAS (80), AVGAS (F18), COMBATGAS (F46)	Not to be used for more than 25 hours; engines rejected 50 hours after first use
	DIESO (F75), DISEO (F76)	
Engine oil:	OX27 (O-156) or OX28	
Mail rotor gearbox:	OEP215, 26-litre	
Intermediate gearbox:	OX26	
Tail rotor gearbox:	OX26	
Hydraulics:	OM15	Undercarriage shock absorbers and hydraulic system
Washer fluid:	AL36	

Topic 10 *The Aircraft Wiring Diagrams*, containing all of the aircraft system circuit diagrams.

With the work carried out, it must be signed for both by the individual who performed the work as well as a supervisor to verify that it has been completed to the required standard. Where airworthiness-related tasks are concerned, such as any work associated with the flying controls, the work must also be physically checked and countersigned for by an independent person – someone who has had no involvement with the work being carried out on that aircraft. These independent checks allow a fresh pair of eyes to inspect the work and hopefully ensure that nothing has been inadvertently missed through over-familiarity with the job in hand.

The details and scope of the work that has been carried out are entered into the aircraft's MoD Form 700 (MF700), which contitutes the maintenance history of the aircraft. It is this document that the Pilot checks through, looking for any system limitations that might affect the sortie and, having been satisfied that all outstanding work and necessary servicing has been carried out, signs to accept the aircraft immediately prior to flight.

Recycling the Lynx

All good things, of course, must come to an end. Although sharing a striking family resemblance, the AgustaWestland AW.159 Wildcat, the first of a total of 62 of which began to replace the Lynx with both the AAC and Royal Marines (as the AH Mk.1) and the Royal Navy (as the HMA Mk.2) from 2013, there is in fact little commonality in terms of the airframe structure – which is completely new.

Nevertheless, many of the aircraft's systems and transmission components have been inherited from its illustrious forebear thanks

BELOW Bearing a striking family resemblance, the AgustaWestland Wildcat HMA Mk.2 (foreground) shares a number of components with the Lynx (background), but in reality is a very much different animal.

of arriving home to RNAS Yeovilton from a lengthy deployment (including humanitarian operations in the Mediterranean), Lynx HMA Mk.8, ZD259 '474/RM', formerly of 815 NAS, 206 Flight, HMS *Richmond*, is loaded aboard a truck ready for despatch to storage and eventual induction into the Wildcat Donor and Strip for Spares Programme.

to a Donor and Strip for Spares Programme that also provides a ready stock of parts to sustain the existing Lynx fleet. This 'harvesting' has seen some 65 common high-price tag components – including main rotor head, main rotor gearbox casing, tail rotor drive shafts, intermediate gearboxes, the composite main rotor blades, main rotor actuators, AFCS computer, fuel and hydraulic systems, deck lock harpoon and SIFF transponder, through to some smaller items such as some of the collective control rods and the tail rotor pedals – carefully removed from the Lynx as they have been withdrawn from service, assessed, repackaged and returned to Yeovil for transplanting back into the Wildcat or back on to the shelves in stores for future reuse.

The wholesale stripping of these once-fine aircraft may seem an ignominious end to some, but it presents a significant saving to the MoD – and the taxpayer – by reducing the amount of wastage and avoiding a great deal of trials and test work that would otherwise have had to have been undertaken to prove any new component designs. It also generates a ready stockpile of spare parts to be used to support and sustain the existing Lynx HMA Mk.8 fleet through to its March 2017 out of service date (OSD). This really is recycling on a grand scale.

Other aircraft in the MoD's inventory benefit too, with items common to the likes of Apache

and Merlin being fed back into the stores system to see another day.

Initial work to strip retired ex-Royal Navy HAS Mk.3 airframes for spares to feed into the Wildcat programme was awarded to the Gazelle Depth Support Hub (GDSH) run by FB Heliservices Ltd at AAC Middle Wallop.

Once stripped of all usable components, the remaining carcasses of the airframes were declared surplus by the MoD Disposals and Sales Agency (DSA) and then disposed of either as ground instruction airframes, gate guardians, museum pieces or sold commercially to the highest bidder either into private collections or ultimately as scrap.

Five ex-Royal Navy Lynx, however, have so far been officially saved for preservation: HAS Mk.3GMS XZ250 in her original 'Black Cats' scheme at Portland Quays – the site of the former HMS *Osprey* (RNAS Portland); HMA Mk.8 XZ692, also in her original 'Black Cats' markings as a gate guardian at HMS *Sultan*, Gosport; HAS Mk.3 XZ699, restored by apprentices at AgustaWestland and reverted back to its original HAS Mk.2 configuration in the Oxford Blue scheme; HAS Mk.3 XZ720, which has the markings it wore while serving aboard HMS *Gloucester* during Operation Granby in 1991; and HMA Mk.8 XZ728, which guards the gate at RNAS Yeovilton. Both XZ699 and XZ720 are now owned by the Fleet Air Arm Museum, RNAS Yeovilton.

LEFT Lynx HAS Mk.3s XZ730 and XZ693, stripped as part of the Wildcat Donor and Strip for Spares Programme. These two examples are seen in the Lynx Operational Support Team (LOST) hangar at RNAS Yeovilton.

CENTRE Death row: a line-up of ex-Royal Navy Lynx HAS Mk.3s awaiting their fate after being sold to a private dealer. Most of these were subsequently scrapped for their metal. *(Alan Allen)*

BELOW Some aircraft have a useful afterlife: in 2015, Lynx HMA Mk.8, XZ719, was unceremoniously dumped at RNAS Yeovilton for crash rescue training by the RNAS Yeovilton fire section.

Chapter Six

Action Lynx!

As an easily deployable small-ships helicopter with over 40 years of service, the Lynx has not surprisingly seen action in a range of varied theatres of operation around the world. From its origins as an anti-submarine helicopter, its versatility has allowed it to undertake a long list of altogether different roles in an ever-changing world.

OPPOSITE Royal Marines fast roping from HMS *Portland*'s Lynx HMA Mk.8, ZF558, onto a dhow suspected of committing piracy in the Indian Ocean during anti-piracy operations in 2009. *(Crown Copyright/LA(Phot) Alex Cave)*

MV *Dubai Moon*
No. 226 Flight HMS *Chatham*,
21 May 2010

On 21 May 2010 the Type 22 frigate HMS *Chatham*, sailing as part of the NATO counter-piracy Operation Ocean Shield in the Indian Ocean, intercepted a distress call from the MV *Dubai Moon*. The 5,786-tonne Panamanian-registered cargo ship had found herself caught in the centre of tropical cyclone Bandu off the coast of Somalia. The violent conditions had caused the merchant ship to roll heavily and her cargo of cars and trucks to break free. At the mercy of the elements and unable to manoeuvre, the ship had listed severely and begun to sink, putting the lives of the 23 crew in real danger.

Conducting any kind of rescue was not going to be an easy task in the prevailing conditions of a sea state 6 and 35–40 knots of wind. Having remained with the vessel for 24 hours as her condition gradually worsened, it became all too clear on board *Chatham* that something had to be done. And soon.

After close consultation with the Commanding Officer, bridge team and flight deck crew, it was judged that the weather had abated sufficiently to allow flying operations. The Lynx was launched with 226 Flight's Flight Commander, Lieutenant Commander Peter Higgins, RN, at the controls, Lieutenant Craig 'Bouncy' Castle, RAN – on an exchange tour from the Royal Australian Navy – as Observer and AET Richard Wilmot as the Winchman in a desperate attempt to recover the 23 crew members before the stricken vessel capsized and sank.

It soon became clear, after the initial airborne recce of the ship, that her cargo of cars and trucks had shifted, causing the *Dubai Moon* to roll from the vertical to 30–40 degrees to starboard and that she was now beginning to sink by the bow. With significant pitching motion and the ship's masts and rigging flailing around, lowering someone to the deck was going to be challenging. Lieutenant Castle quickly determined that there was a small area immediately aft of the superstructure in which it would just be possible to put the Winchman on to the heaving deck.

As the aircraft buffeted severely in the

BELOW Lynx HMA Mk.8, ZF563 '348/CM', of 815 NAS, 226 Flight, named 'Semper Perturbo' and carrying nose art on arrival back at RNAS Yeovilton from HMS *Chatham* after the MV *Dubai Moon* rescue.

turbulence caused by the impact of the gale-force winds against the slab-sided superstructure, Lieutenant Commander Higgins fought to maintain a steady hover, using external references that were limited by poor visibility, over the transfer point with the aid of a calm, accurate and detailed 'con' from Lieutenant Castle. This really was operating at the very edge of the aircraft's flying envelope!

The oily conditions and angle of the deck on MV *Dubai Moon* meant that a normal winch or hi-line recovery would not be possible, forcing Lieutenant Commander Higgins to reassess the rapidly changing situation and make a series of quick but crucial decisions to ensure that the risk to his crew was kept to a minimum, while still being able to carry out the mission. With Lieutenant Castle now occupying the rear cabin, Higgins now found himself not only as the Pilot but as the aircraft commander, meaning that he had to make these decisions while dividing his attention between flying, maintaining communications and while reacting to Lieutenant Castle's con as he relayed details of the developing scenario on the deck below. This required immense concentration, close teamwork and careful prioritisation in a tense and critical situation.

For AET Wilmot, this was to be his first live winching serial from the aircraft following his qualifying course. A real baptism of fire, if ever there was one! Having been attached to the winch wire and lowered to the deck, it was immediately apparent that it was covered in a thick layer of oil which, combined with the sea water cascading over the side, produced a lethal, slippery emulsion that meant it was impossible to stand up. Wilmot attempted to take hold of the windward handrail but was unable to maintain his hold and slid down the steep and oily deck, caught only by the winch wire he was attached to. It was an impossible situation and so he was winched back up to the aircraft.

The flight crew quickly agreed that there were no other suitable winching points and that the only option was to attempt to recover the stricken crew with a modified winching technique. The crew of the *Dubai Moon* were instructed to lay a rope on deck, secured to the windward rail, and AET Wilmot was lowered

back down close to where the rope lay. Once on deck, he managed to take hold of the rope and pulled himself up to where the first of the crewmen to be rescued was located. He secured the crewman in the double-lift strop and then moved down the improvised recovery rope, ensuring they both passed clear of obstructions before being winched back into the aircraft.

For any seasoned Winchman these would be challenging circumstances; for Wilmot, who had insisted that he had overcome a bout of seasickness that he had been suffering from for the preceding 36 hours, his weakened physical condition combined with the extreme physical exertion proved to be too much and on return to the aircraft he was violently sick. Clearly it was impossible for him to continue with the mission.

Though his role in the rescue had been cut short, his undeterred actions on deck had saved the first life, but more importantly it had established the improvised method and prepared the crew of the ship for the remainder of this hazardous and highly challenging rescue operation.

He demonstrated courage, resilience and grit to an extent that is unexpected and highly commendable in someone so junior and with no operational experience as a Winchman. Having only flown for 5 hours 30 minutes prior to the rescue, the manner in which he took control of the situation on the deck of MV *Dubai Moon* in extremely challenging circumstances was outstanding and set the conditions for success.

As luck would have it, visiting HMS *Chatham* at the time on a ship operational airworthiness audit on behalf of Navy Command Headquarters was Lieutenant Commander Graham Chesterman. Although a qualified Lynx Observer, Chesterman had not actually flown for 15 years and, despite considerable aviation experience, he had never acted as Winchman in a rescue mission. But, during the pre-mission planning, one of the contingencies that had been considered was to use him as a stand-in Winchman should there be unforeseen problems in this predictably difficult rescue.

With Chesterman having been given a thorough brief and handover by Wilmot of the situation that would be encountered on the deck of *Dubai Moon*, the aircraft relaunched. During the next 3 hours Chesterman conducted a total of 22 difficult and physically exhausting transfers to bring the rest of the crew to safety. His performance was superb, fighting to recover the crew from a deck that by now was perilously strewn with debris, slick with a thick film of oil and sea water and rolling by up to 40 degrees. This selfless act of bravery and physical endurance was all the more impressive as the leeward guard rails had been destroyed and a mistake on his part would have resulted in the death of any one of the seamen had they fallen over board. His fearless composure galvanised the Aircraft Commander and crew, while reassuring the survivors who placed their lives – quite literally – in his hands. Despite the marginal weather conditions, the hazardous state of the deck and the dangerous pitch and roll of a vessel on the verge of sinking, all crew members were safely recovered to HMS *Chatham*.

The courage, sense of duty, stamina and professionalism in extraordinary circumstances ensured that the lives of all 23 crewmen were saved. Within 10 hours of completing the mission, MV *Dubai Moon* sank.

For his part in the operation, Lieutenant Commander Peter Higgins, RN, was awarded the Air Force Cross; Lieutenant Commander Graham Chesterman, RN, received the Queen's Commendation for Bravery Award, while the whole of the crew, including Lieutenant Craig 'Bouncy' Castle, RAN, and AET Richard Wilmot, were awarded the Prince Philip Helicopter Rescue Award by the Guild of Air Pilots and Air Navigators and the Edward and Maisie Lewis Award by the Shipwrecked Fisherman & Mariners' Royal Benevolent Society.

Counter-piracy operations

One of the major roles performed by the Lynx HMA Mk.8 in the final decade of its service has been counter-piracy. Some 90% of the world's traded materials are moved by sea and approximately 40% of this passes through the Indian Ocean, the Gulf of Aden and the Arabian Sea. Since 2008, the Royal Navy has maintained a presence in these areas to help police the oceans and keep passing shipping safe from the threat of attack from Somali pirates, intent on taking control of vessels carrying precious cargo, holding their crews hostage and demanding ransoms for their release.

As an island nation, the scourge of piracy poses a threat to the economy and security of the United Kingdom. Banking, insurance and shipping industries are all affected by the loss of vital goods. In 2007 there had been 55 attempted and successful hijackings; by 2009 this had risen to 219 with 3,500 seafarers taken hostage and 62 people killed. In the first three months of 2011 some 97 attacks had been made against shipping off Somalia – an average of one per day. By this stage somewhere in the region of 1,500–3,000 pirates were thought to be operating off the Somali coast and, by the end of 2011, ransoms of $135 million had been paid.

Counter-piracy ops à la française – Lieutenant Mike Curd, RN, ex-217 Flight Commander, 815 Naval Air Squadron

It is 6 January 2013, just after dawn. A fat, searingly hot orange sun is rising rapidly over the Indian Ocean some 200 miles east of Somalia. The heat increases perceptibly with every degree it rises on its arc. A long, low white skiff is charging across the waves in the direction of the coast, its two occupants sweating in the humidity. And in fear. They are pirates, fleeing the scene of an attempted attack on a merchant vessel the day before. In a desperate bid to escape, they have abandoned ten of their countrymen in a heavier, slower whaler somewhere to the west. But their flight is in vain.

The unmistakable drone of a Lynx HMA Mk.8 cuts through the air and suddenly they can see it, sweeping in fast from their right. The outline of the .50 calibre M3M heavy machine gun is equally unmistakable. The skiff stops and the Lynx moves to cover it in a slow orbit. For a minute, one of the pirates half-heartedly mimes the act of fishing, but then sits down heavily – the game is up.

In total, 12 suspected pirates were arrested that day and later passed to the Mauritian authorities for successful prosecution; another great success for the Fleet Air Arm and the venerable Lynx but, at first glance, not necessarily that remarkable. Lynx Flights have routinely been deployed in and round the Indian Ocean, taking part in counter-piracy (CP) operations, for years. But the HMA Mk.8 in this particular story was not embarked in a Royal Navy vessel, nor even an RFA. This 815 NAS Lynx was from 217 Flight, deployed in FLF *Surcouf*, of France's Marine Nationale.

A French ship? What would Nelson think? What on earth were the Fleet Air Arm's finest doing working hand-in-hand with the 'Old Enemy'? The successful CP operation described here was the tangible result of a treaty signed in 2010 between the UK and France, agreeing to greater military cooperation and interoperability between the two countries. As a result, 217 Flight was chosen to detach for five months in the La Fayette class *frégate Surcouf*. The Flight's two aircrew (myself as the Flight Commander/Observer, and my Pilot, Lieutenant Chris Southworth), eight maintainers and two Royal Marine snipers were to deploy with the ship for Operation Atalanta, the EU Naval Force (EUNAVFOR) CP mission in the Indian Ocean.

It is fair to say that the challenges of planning and conducting such an embarkation were many and varied but, by late November 2012, we had flown our Lynx – named 'Miss Fit', tail number ZD252 – and shipped a total of 4 tonnes of equipment across the length of France to join the ship in Toulon, from where we set sail to join task force (TF) 465 and the EUNAVFOR mission.

The Atalanta mission itself was broadly twofold: detection, deterrence and disruption of piracy activities; and protection of World Food Programme and other vulnerable shipping. To achieve these goals there were three main areas in which the Lynx was used during our time in the task force; surface search/patrol, intelligence surveillance and reconnaissance (ISR) along the Somali coast and the interception of vessels suspected of being involved in piracy.

While the capture and detention of suspected pirates such as described here was the 'punchy' and headline-grabbing end of the EUNAVFOR mission, it was only the tip of a very big iceberg. The majority of our time was spent conducting 'baseline' counter-piracy

tasking. Usually flying at dawn and again at dusk, we participated in constant surveillance of the international recommended transit corridor (IRTC) in the Gulf of Aden, performing the 'bread and butter' Lynx task of compilation of the recognised maritime picture (RMP).

On these searches, we usually chose to carry just one of our Maritime Sniper Team (MST) sniper pair. This was a trade-off between aircraft performance and what we expected to use the sniper for during the sortie. While two heads are often better than one (especially where Royal Marines are concerned!), we were often at the limit of available power for the conditions due to the ambient heat. Carrying an extra crew member would have meant reducing our fuel load, which in turn would reduce our time on task. Once we'd taken into account the weight of the M3M gun, ammunition, camera gear, automatic identification system (AIS) laptop and other mission-related equipment, the addition of another stocky Marine would have seriously hampered our range and therefore utility.

The recent addition to the Lynx of the AIS laptop really was a boon for these types of searches. Using the laptop in coordination with the radar, we could rapidly build up the surface picture (i.e. the shipping around us)

ABOVE A Lynx of 815 NAS, 217 Flight, crewed by Lieutenants Mike Curd and Chris Southworth, and CPO Matthew 'Cakey' Eccles, flying off the French frigate FLF *Surcouf,* aids the capture of suspected pirates during Operation Atalanta in March 2013.
(Crown Copyright)

ABOVE No. 815
NAS, 217 Flight,
personnel, including
Lieutenant Mike
Curd, RN, (standing,
second from right)
after being presented
with the Fleet Air
Arm's coveted Osprey
Trophy in recognition
of their outstanding
contribution during
operations in
FLF *Surcouf*.
*(Crown Copyright/
L(Phot) Abbie Herron)*

and identify easily which contacts warranted further investigation. For the uninitiated, every ship over a certain size must, by law, transmit a raft of information on AIS. Those without an AIS 'signature' were instantly highlighted to us as being of interest, and thus we could search a large area very efficiently.

Far more interesting than these surface searches, however, was the significant amount of coastal ISR tasking we carried out. Along huge stretches of the north and north-east coast of Somalia were scattered a multitude of camps, villages and small towns that were, or could easily become, logistical bases for pirates. Only by keeping a constant watch on these areas could the 'pattern of life' be established and any suspicious activity spotted. Dawn and dusk patrols, armed with a high-resolution DSLR camera and sufficiently long lens, allowed us to distinguish between routine activities such as fishing or fuel trading and indicators of possible pirate action group (PAG) preparation ashore.

Surface search and ISR came firmly under the detection and deterrence part of the Atalanta mission and were extremely routine in nature. On 5 January 2012, I was summoned

to the ops room and told we would finally be used for disruption. A container ship, the MSC *Jasmine*, had successfully repulsed an armed attack and the pirates had fled the scene in two boats. A combined multinational effort including a Swedish maritime patrol aircraft (MPA) and US Navy destroyer had subsequently detected and followed the boats that were believed to be those that had attacked the *Jasmine*.

Enter the Lynx!

Dawn broke on 6 January fine and clear and the day rapidly became hot and humid as the sun rose. We launched to relocate the first of the two boats: a fast-moving skiff. Despite having a good estimated position from the units that had been recently tracking it and despite the power and definition of the Lynx's *Seaspray* radar, the tiny skiff was not at all easy to spot! However, we soon had it in our sights and gradually inched closer to begin the process of bringing it to a halt.

Rather than flying right up to the boat gung-ho style, all guns blazing, the approach was a careful process of hazard identification and risk mitigation, using imaging equipment at distance to look for any weapons that could pose a threat to the aircraft and warning the boat's occupants that we were approaching and required them to stop. With the M3M machine gun prepared – for self-defence and, if required, to fire warning shots – and manned by a Royal Marine not long returned from seeing active service in Afghanistan, the Flight Commander's job at this point was to strike the right balance of a measured, yet purposeful approach. After weeks and weeks of routine flying and 'groundhog day' searches of mostly empty ocean, the temptation to get a bit over-excited can be very real.

After trying to contact the boat using the aircraft's radio, then with hand signals or a large printed 'STOP' sign held up by the guys in the back, the warnings process could be escalated to a shot across the bow (SATB) with the M3M. Not only is the gun extremely loud, the .50 calibre rounds hitting the water throw up plumes about 30ft in height; the combined effect is intimidating to say the least!

If, after SATB, the occupants of the skiff are still feeling brave or stupid enough to continue trying to escape, the sniper's day is really made! Disabling fire (DF) into the motor of the boat is not only extremely effective but genuinely frightening in its accuracy.

However, escalation to SATB and DF requires putting the aircraft within range of any weapons on board the boat that may have been hidden during our previous examination, and is therefore very much a last resort. Fortunately for us (perhaps disappointingly for my snipers), the skiff stopped almost immediately we began our approach and we could back off again to a covering orbit to maintain watch while the ship caught up with the action.

While we were relocating and stopping the skiff, the *Surcouf* was heading towards us at full speed and preparing her boarding teams. The next phase required perfect coordination between the Lynx, the ship and her two sea-boats (very fast rigid-hulled inflatable boats – RHIBs) to effect a safe transition to control by the boarding teams for the arrest of the suspected pirates (SPs) – not an easy task when conducted in a foreign language! The months of training with the ship before the mission paid off, however, and while our snipers covered the skiff from above with yet another weapon in their arsenal – an anti-personnel

capability (a euphemism if ever there was one) – the sea-boats moved in and seamlessly took charge of the boat and its occupants.

Once the boarding team had control of the boat and SPs the Lynx's job was over, and so we returned to *Surcouf* to refuel and prepare to repeat the entire process for the second boat, the whaler. By the end of the day, 12 SPs had been arrested and 'Miss Fit' had played a central role at every stage.

She may have been old and in her twilight years, but given the chance to do what she does best, the Lynx excels … even when working in French!

MV *Montecristo*
229 Flight, RFA *Fort Victoria*, October 2011 – Lieutenant Andrew Henderson, RN

It was while deployed in RFA *Fort Victoria* in late 2011 that the ship's embarked Lynx HMA Mk.8 aided in the capture of a total of no fewer than 47 Somali pirates who were threatening shipping in the Indian Ocean. Lieutenant Andrew Henderson, 229 Flight's Observer at the time, recalls one of those intercepts:

It was just before 5.00am on the morning of Monday 10 October 2011 when the coalition forces that made up the NATO counter-piracy mission Operation Ocean Shield patrolling the Indian Ocean discovered, of all things, a message in a bottle floating in the sea. The bottle had been strapped to a flashing beacon and thrown from the top of the funnel of the Italian-flagged MV *Montecristo*. The 56,000-ton bulk carrier, which had left Liverpool on 20 September bound for Vietnam with a cargo of scrap iron, reported that they had been attacked by pirates some 620nm east of the coast of Somalia and the multinational crew of 23 had fled to the vessel's armoured safe room – the 'citadel' – which was designed for use in just such an event. In fact the ship was so new, having been launched in June of that year, that it had been built with all of the latest anti-piracy measures included in the design. But despite the standard anti-piracy tactics of firing water cannon at the attackers and draping barbed wire along the sides of the ships, the pirates had succeeded in getting on board.

ABOVE With RFA
Fort Victoria's Lynx
HMA Mk.8 hovering
overhead and the USS
De Wert alongside,
the MV *Montecristo*
and her crew are freed
from pirates,
11 October 2011.
*(Crown Copyright/
LA(Phot) Dave Jenkins)*

Shipping in this part of the Indian Ocean had become the target of many Somali pirate gangs over the past few years. Operating from so-called 'motherships', these gangs would board vessels from fast-moving skiffs. Armed with Ak-47 rifles and rocket-propelled grenades (RPGs), they would take the ships by force and hold the crews and cargo for ransom, earning themselves millions of dollars in the process. It was a growing problem; dozens of ships and hundreds of crew members had fallen victim to these lawless desperados.

Although the crew of the *Montecristo* could continue to control the ship's steering while holed up in the ship's safe room within the engine room, all further communications had been lost when the attackers had destroyed the radio equipment on board, preventing the crew from sending out a more traditional mayday call. In order to determine the best way to go about retaking the ship and freeing its crew without, hopefully, loss of life, the situation had first to be fully determined. With the *Montecristo* some 100nm away, the quickest way to do that was to send the ship's Lynx.

No. 229 Flight, parented by 815 Naval Air Squadron, had arrived in theatre about a month before and had sailed from Dubai in RFA *Fort Victoria* to the Indian Ocean. By the time we arrived, both the ship and the Flight were fully worked-up and ready for action. Under the direction of Captain Shawn Jones OBE RN, the ship's Commanding Officer, and Captain Gerry Northwood RN, the aircraft was called to Alert 5 to be ready to launch and intercept the vessel. Briefings took place in the ship's operations room and a plan was made based on the capabilities of the Lynx aircraft. As ever, the weather was hot, humid and dusty. The Lynx, with its numerous modifications through

LEFT *Fort Victoria*'s Lynx displays its .50-cal M3M machine gun. *(Crown Copyright/LA(Phot) Dave Jenkins)*

the years had become considerably heavier than it was originally designed to be and, with the searingly hot temperatures of between 35 and 40°C, she was only just able to launch with a full fuel load and crew of two: myself and the Pilot, Lieutenant A.J. Thompson.

We intercepted at range, operating by that stage some 100nm from *Fort Victoria* and the only available landing site for around 500nm, well outside of the aircraft's range. The tell-tale signs were plain to see as we surveyed the ship from a safe distance with visible damage to the bridge of the ship caused by grenade launchers. This was indeed a hijack situation; the ship was now in the hands of pirates.

Having managed to determine the status of the ship and – as far as possible – the crew, and having then relayed the information by radio to the operations team, we quickly headed back to *Fort Victoria* to refuel and await the next part of the operation which would take several hours to plan and position for. With the ship's top speed being around 15 knots, it was slow going, but the intercept was calculated and achieved capably by the navigating officer and deck officers.

It took an overnight 'sprint' by the ship to get into position, but once in visual range *Fort Victoria* launched her Royal Marines boarding teams in ballistic-protected Pacific 24 RIBs while we in the Lynx helicopter with our .50 cal M3M machine gun and MST – armed with powerful Heckler & Koch G3KA4 7.62mm anti-material marksman and L121A1 anti-material bolt action 12.7mm rifles – maintained an overwatch of the proceedings on board to ensure the Royal Marines were safe as they made their boarding onto the *Montecristo*.

From our lofty vantage point we had by far the best view of the action on board. As we watched, the Royal Marines sped across the ocean to the *Montecristo* and quickly made their boarding. Having seen the overwhelming Royal Navy force heading towards them and realising that the Royal Marines would quickly get the better of them, the pirates had, rather sensibly, lost their appetite for a further fight for the vessel and quickly gave themselves up without a single shot being fired. Eleven Somali pirates were found on board and taken into custody. The crew of the vessel were freed

RECENT ROYAL NAVY LYNX HMA MK.8 OPERATIONS AND COMMITMENTS

Atlantic Patrol Tasking (South)
APT(S) is a permanent Royal Navy presence maintained in the South Atlantic and covering the vast area between West Africa, the Falkland Islands and South Georgia to protect British interests, especially the sovereignty of the latter. In more recent times the tasking has seen frigates and destroyers equipped with the Lynx HMA Mk.8 venture as far east as the Pacific Ocean.

Atlantic Patrol Tasking (North)
Formerly known as the West Indies Guard Ship, APT(N) provides reassurance to UK overseas dependent territories in the North Atlantic and Caribbean, providing humanitarian and disaster relief during the main hurricane season (June to November) and conducting counter-narcotic patrols as part of the wider international effort.

Operation Kipion
Following the Iran/Iraq War of 1980, Royal Navy and Royal Fleet Auxiliary ships were sent to maintain a patrol in the Persian Gulf to protect British interests under the operational name of the Armilla Patrol. Still maintaining this role, but now with coverage extended further south to the coast of Somalia to protect international shipping from the threat of piracy, it is has since been retitled as Operation Kipion. Royal Navy frigates and destroyers equipped with the Lynx have seen action here aided by Royal Fleet Auxiliary ships, which have also occasionally had their own embarked Lynx Flight.

Standing Naval Response Force Maritime Group 1
Standing Naval Response Force Maritime Group 1 (SNRFMG1) is a multinational naval group that is permanently assigned to NATO, providing the NATO alliance with the ability to respond quickly to crisis situations anywhere in the world. Among its wide range of potential missions are non-combatant evacuations, counter-terrorism, crisis response and embargo operations.

Fleet Ready Escort
The Fleet Ready Escort is a frigate or destroyer maintained by the Royal Navy anywhere in the world at a high state of readiness, fully prepared to be deployed as required at short notice.

Combined Task Force 150 (CTF 150)
Maritime security and counter-terrorism operations.

Combined Task Force 151
US-led maritime counter-piracy operations, taking over from CTF 150, actively deterring, disrupting and suppressing piracy to protect global maritime security and secure freedom of navigation for the benefit of all nations.

ABOVE Royal Navy and Royal Marine Commandos board a Somalian whaler suspected of being operated by pirates in the Indian Ocean off the Horn of Africa. A Lynx from RFA *Fort Victoria* (in the background) identified two suspect vessels, a whaler and a skiff, and gave chase. *(Crown Copyright/ LA(Phot) Dave Jenkins)*

unharmed from inside their safe room and the now-secured vessel was escorted to Italy for minor repairs to the bridge before continuing on its passage. The pirates were handed over to the Italian Navy (as the *Montecristo* fell under Italian jurisdiction), and were eventually prosecuted for piracy on the high seas.

It might have been a happy end for the crew of the *Montecristo*, but for those of us back on RFA *Fort Victoria* the job was still far from done. Continuing our operations in the Indian Ocean, we later intercepted a large fishing dhow which was believed to have been used as the mothership for the piracy attack against the *Montecristo*. For this action we teamed up with HMS *Somerset* and her embarked Merlin helicopter to conduct a successful boarding and capture of the vessel and suspected pirates.

Counter-narcotics operations

One of the Royal Navy's main operations is Atlantic Patrol Tasking (North). As well as helping to provide humanitarian assistance during the hurricane season, operating in the warm waters of the Caribbean also brings the Lynx HMA Mk.8s embarked in either Type

23 frigates or Type 45 destroyers into direct contact with drug smugglers plying the oceans with their illegal cargoes.

Cocaine haul in the Caribbean – Lieutenant Jonny Hamlyn, RN, 211 Flight, HMS *Argyll*

It was summer 2014. I say 'summer'; for the past few months we had been in the northern hemisphere conducting APT(N) duties around the Caribbean from Key West in the north, as far west as Vera Cruz, Mexico, south as Cartagena, Colombia, and as far east as the Leeward Islands. While back home in the UK everyone was sweltering in the heat, we had been 'enjoying' what would in fact be effectively a continuous summer that year and a seemingly endless round of port visits to host local dignitaries and meet with local authorities and military leaders.

And so it was perhaps understandably with some relief that in July we finally bade the area a fond farewell as HMS *Argyll* turned around to begin our return trip home with the promise of much-needed leave after what would be seven very long months at sea.

It had been a busy period in the Caribbean: a period which had seen us already carry out three drugs busts as well as being involved in humanitarian work in the immediate aftermath of tropical cyclone Joaquin which had passed near to Bermuda on 4 October. Thankfully by that stage it had weakened and had not done as much damage as had initially been feared. Our Lynx was quickly put to use conducting aerial surveys, allowing local engineers to inspect the damage to overhead power lines as well as carrying out helicopter delivery service (HDS) duties.

And now, here we were on our final day of counter-narcotics duties patrolling the Caribbean: drug baron territory. And they were out there.

Having received details of a suspected drug smuggler attempting to cross the Caribbean, HMS *Argyll* set off on a lengthy overnight sprint to arrive in a position just over the horizon from where the suspect boat was racing through the water. Actioning ZD268, roled with an MST and – as we were in effect operating under American jurisdiction – a US Coast Guard airborne use of force (AUF) controller in the back for a surface search and interception, we had around an hour left until sunset, whereupon a successful interdiction would have been impossible.

After launching from *Argyll*'s flight deck we climbed and within a short time had made visual contact with a large wake consistent with a small boat making high speed towards nearby territorial waters. Remaining downwind and up-sun to minimise the chance of being heard or spotted, ZD268 ran in up the boat's stern and executed a fast-stop manoeuvre to starboard to leave the suspect vessel down in our 4 o'clock position. The occupants of the boat were clearly not going to give up without a fight as they ignored the visual 'STOP!' signals being given by the guys in the cabin and all attempts to hail them on the maritime VHF radio frequency failed. It was time to get serious and fire some warning shots across their bow using the potent M3M gun. Despite having a hail of bullets rain down all around them, the boat still failed to stop. There was only one way these guys were going to be halted: the use of non-lethal disabling fire. Armed with their .50 calibre sniper rifles, the MST in the cabin took careful aim at the boat's outboard motors and fired.

First one engine, then the second; finally all three of the engines were shot out and the boat began to slow until it was eventually stopped in the water. The game was up.

Hovering close by to await *Argyll*'s arrival on the scene with their US Coast Guard boarding team, we kept careful watch at a safe distance. As we did so, the two occupants of the boat began to bring out their expensive cargo, wrapped in black polythene and held together with yellow tape. One by one, the drug runners proceeded to carefully tie rope around each parcel in a sort of daisy chain before hauling the whole lot over the side. Clearly their expectation was for the bundles to sink before the ship arrived and had chance to capture the evidence. To our amusement, however, we watched as the packages floated away from the boat in a nice, neatly held-together string. You could see the disappointment on the boat occupants' faces.

It had been an eventful and satisfying final day. As we returned to *Argyll* there was time to reflect on the part we – and our Lynx – had played in the seizure of a haul of 250kg of pure cocaine: drugs that we had helped to stop from entering the worldwide illegal narcotics market.

ABOVE Meaning business! An Observer armed with the M3M gun and a member of the MST taking aim at the bad guys. *(Crown Copyright/LA(Phot) Ian 'Simmo' Simmonds)*

Appendices

Lynx HAS Mk.2, HAS Mk.3 and HMA Mk.8 operating units

No. 700L Naval Air Squadron, RNAS Yeovilton, September 1976–December 1977; July 1990–July 1992.

No. 702 Naval Air Squadron, RNAS Portland, July 1982–January 1999.

No. 702 Naval Air Squadron, RNAS Yeovilton, January 1978–July 1982; January 1999–August 2014.

No. 815 Naval Air Squadron, RNAS Yeovilton, January 1981–July 1982; February 1999–March 2017.

No. 815 Naval Air Squadron, RNAS Portland, July 1982–February 1999.

No. 829 Naval Air Squadron, RNAS Portland, September 1986–March 1993.

BELOW Not quite what it seems. In 2011, Lynx HAS Mk.3GMS, XZ233 '635' of 702 NAS, was refinished in the Oxford Blue scheme originally applied to the HAS Mk.2 variant when it first entered service in 1976 with 700L NAS.

Lynx HMA Mk.8 leading particulars

Date entered service:	1994
Length:	50ft (15.24m) (spread); 35ft 7in (10.854m) (folded)
Height:	12ft (3.65m) (spread); 10ft 6in (3.25m) (folded)
Width:	9ft 8in (2.94m) (folded)
Main rotor span:	42ft (12.802m)
Basic weight:	7,988lb (3,623kg)
Maximum all-up mass:	11,750lb (5,330kg)
Endurance:	2 hours 10 minutes (unarmed ASW/maritime patrol role)
Cruising speed	120 knots
Max speed:	143 knots
Max range:	260nm
Crew:	2
Passengers:	7

ABOVE When knowing the dimensions of the aircraft become all-important: Lynx HMA Mk.8, ZD259, being airfreighted in a C-17 aircraft to Basra, Iraq, in 2004 to join 815 NAS, 204 Flight, aboard HMS *Norfolk*.
(Jack Gibbs)

Selected examples of Lynx HMA Mk.8 counter-piracy, counter-narcotic and humanitarian operations since 2007

BELOW Lynx HMA Mk.8, ZF558 '426', of 815 NAS, 234 Flight, from HMS *Portland* intercepting and boarding one of two suspicious skiffs during counter piracy operations in the Gulf of Aden, 2 June 2009. Items were subsequently found on board indicating that the vessel had been involved in (or was about to conduct an act of) piracy.
(LA(Phot) Alex Cave/ Crown Copyright)

Between January 2007 and 2011 the Royal Navy assigned 12 vessels solely to Operations Telic, Calash and Kipion (EU and NATO counter-terrorist/counter-piracy operations in the Persian Gulf and off the coast of Somalia). A further 23 participated while en route to or from other missions.

Other operations that have involved the Lynx HMA Mk.8 in recent years have been Unified Protector (Libya, 2011), Ocean Shield (anti-piracy, Gulf of Aden/Indian Ocean), Martillo (15-nation effort to prevent drug-trafficking by sea or air in the Central and South America region) and Patwin (typhoon Haiyan humanitarian relief work in the Philippines).

The following are just a few selected examples of some of the operations in which the embarked Lynx HMA Mk.8s of 815 NAS's small-ship Flights have been involved. It is by no means complete, but gives an illustration of the aircraft's use outside UK waters.

Counter-piracy operations:
2009
No. 815 NAS 234/*Portland* Flt (ZF558), CTF151, assisted with the interception and boarding of two skiffs suspected to be involved in piracy in the Gulf of Aden.

2011
No. 815 NAS 215/*Monmouth* Flt (XZ725), Operation Calash, helped to thwart hijack on 63,000-tonne bulk carrier MV *Caravos Horizon* in the Red Sea.

No. 815 NAS 229/RFA *Fort Victoria* Flt, 11 October 2011 (ZF562), assisted in the rescue of the crew of Italian bulk carrier MV *Montecristo* from attack by pirates; 11 pirates captured.

No. 815 NAS 229/RFA *Fort Victoria* Flt, 28 November 2011 (ZF562), assisted with deterring pirates from attacking Spanish fishing vessel

500m off the Seychelles in the Indian Ocean as part of CTF508. Whaler and skiff captured along with seven pirates.

2012
No. 815 NAS 229/RFA *Fort Victoria* Flt (ZF562), assisted with prevention chemical tanker MV *Liquid Velvet* under control of Somali pirates in Indian Ocean from reaching the Gulf of Aden.

No. 815 NAS 229/RFA *Fort Victoria* Flt (ZF562), assisted with the retaking of a dhow captured earlier by Somali pirates in the Gulf of Aden.

2013
No. 815 NAS 217/FLF *Surcouf* Flt (ZD252), thwarted attack by pirates on MSC *Jasmine* in the Indian Ocean off Somalia.

No. 815 NAS 214/*Montrose* Flt (ZF562), thwarted attack by pirates on tanker MV *Al Safliya* in the Persian Gulf.

Counter-narcotics operations:
2007
No. 815 NAS 206/*Portland* Flt, Venezuelan fishing vessel intercepted at dawn, leading to the capture of 2.5 tons of cocaine.

2013
No. 815 NAS 202/*Lancaster* Flt (ZD257), 204 cannabis plants seized from a plantation in Anguilla.

No. 815 NAS 202/*Lancaster* Flt (ZD257), 680kg of pure cocaine seized from a small boat off Puerto Rico.

No. 815 NAS 202/*Lancaster* Flt (ZD257), helped to seize £55 million of cocaine and £3 million of marijuana in the Caribbean during Operation Martillo.

2014
No. 815 NAS 211/*Argyll* Flt (ZD268), 600kg of cocaine (worth £21 million) seized from 'go-fast' boat south of Santo Domingo, Dominican Republic.

No. 815 NAS 211/*Argyll* Flt (ZD268), seized £10 million of cocaine from a yacht in the Caribbean.

2015
No. 815 NAS 206/*Richmond* Flt (ZD259), assisted with stopping a drug-smuggling boat in the Mediterranean with £3 million (1,015kg) of cannabis on board.

Humanitarian assistance operations:
2010
No. 815 NAS 226/*Chatham* Flt (ZF563), rescued the 23 crew members of the merchant ship MV *Dubai Moon* off Somalia.

2013
No. 815 NAS 200/*Daring* Flt (ZD259), assistance following typhoon Haiyan in the Philippines (Operation Patwin).

2015
No. 815 NAS 206/*Richmond* Flt (ZD259), assisted with the Safety of Life at Sea (SOLAS) in Mediterranean as part of European naval efforts to stop migrant crisis between North Africa and Europe (Operation Sofia).

ABOVE Lynx HMA Mk.8, ZD259 '474/ RM', of 815 NAS, 206 Flight, on board HMS *Richmond* during Operation Sophia in the Mediterranean. Boats containing a total of 101 people had been intercepted off the north coast of Africa as part of the European maritime effort to stem the migrant crisis between Africa and Europe, 28 October 2015. *(LA(Phot) Luron Wright/ Crown Copyright)*

Glossary

AAC	Army Air Corps
ACMN	Aircrewman
ADG	Air Door Gunner
AEW	Airborne Early Warning
AFC	Air Force Cross
AFM	Air Force Medal
AFS	After Flight Servicing
AMG	Aircraft Maintenance Group
AS	Anti-Submarine
AUF	Airborne Use of Force
AW	AgustaWestland
BERP	British Experimental Rotor Programme
BFS	Before Flight Servicing
BS381C	British standard for paint
Cab	Slang term for aircraft
CASEVAC	Casualty Evacuation
CofG	Centre of Gravity
CPO	Chief Petty Officer
D1	Depth 1 maintenance cycle
D2	Depth 2 maintenance cycle
DSP	Digital Signal Processor
EGV	Exit Guide Vane
EOMS	Electro-Optic Missile Sensors
ESM	Electronic Support Measures
FLF	*Frégate Légère Furtive*
Flt	Flight
FRE	Fleet Ready Escort
GE	General Electric
GM	George Medal
GRP	Glass Reinforced Plastic
HAR	Helicopter Air Rescue
HAS	Helicopter Anti-Submarine
HMA	Helicopter Maritime Attack
HMS	His/Her Majesty's Ship
HP	High Pressure
HU	Helicopter Utility
IGB	Intermediate Gearbox
IGV	Inlet Guide Vane
JNAST	Joint Navy/Air Staff Target
kg	Kilogram
lb	Pounds (weight)
LEDET	Law Enforcement Detachment
LHTEC	Light Helicopter Turbine Engine Company
LP	Low Pressure
LSJ	Life-Saving Jacket
LUH	Light Utility Helicopter
MAD	Magnetic Anomaly Detection
Mk	Mark
MoD	Ministry of Defence
MoS	Ministry of Supply
MST	Maritime Sniper Team
NAD	Naval Air Department
NAS	Naval Air Squadron
NATO	North Atlantic Treaty Organization
Nf	Freewheel rotational speed
Ng	Engine gas turbine rotational speed
NGAST	Naval, General and Air Staff Target
Nh	Gas generator speed
nm	Nautical miles
Nr	Main rotor speed
NSR	Naval Staff Requirement
NVD	Night Vision Device
OEP	Oil Extreme Pressure
OM	Oil Mineral (heavy-duty engine oil)
OMD	Oil Mineral Dispersant
OR	Operational Requirement
OX	Synthetic oil
PID	Passive Identification Device
PO	Petty Officer
POB	Persons on Board
PX	Corrosion preventative oil
RADAR	Radio Detection and Ranging
RAF	Royal Air Force
RAN	Royal Australian Navy
RFTG	Response Force Task Group
RIB	Rigid-hulled Inflatable Boat
RM	Royal Marines
RN	Royal Navy
RNAS	Royal Naval Air Station
RPG	Rocket-Propelled Grenade
RRHT	Rolls-Royce Heritage Trust
SACRU	Semi-Automatic Cargo Release Unit
SAR	Search and Rescue
SARBE	Search and Rescue Beacon
SATURN	Second-generation Tactical UHF Radio for NATO
shp	shaft horse power
Sitrep	Situation report
SNIAS	Société Nationale Industrielle Aérospatiale
SONAR	Sound Navigation and Ranging
STASS	Short-Term Air Supply System
TR	Turn-round Flight servicing
TRDS	Tail Rotor Driveshaft
UOR	Urgent Operational Requirement
USCG	United States Coast Guard
WAL	Westland Aircraft Ltd
WHL	Westland Helicopters Ltd
WO1	Warrant Officer First Class

Sources

Uttley, Matthew, *Westland and the British Helicopter Industry 1945-1960 – Licensed Production versus Indigenous Innovation* (Frank Cass Publishers, 2001)

James, Derek N., *Westland Aircraft since 1915* (Putnam, 1991)

Falklands – the Air War (British Aviation Research Group, 1986)

Howard, Lee, Burrow, Mick and Myall, Eric, *Fleet Air Arm Helicopters since 1943* (Air-Britain, 2011)

Ballance, Theo, Sturtivant, Ray and Howard, Lee, *The Squadrons and Units of the Fleet Air Arm* (Air-Britain, 2016)

BELOW Lynx HMA Mk.8, ZD257 '302/VL', of 815 NAS HQ Flight perched high up on the snowy slopes of Mount Snowdon during mountain flying training in Wales, 15 March 2016.

Index